"The Golden Helmet" and "The Green Helmet"

Manuscript Materials

THE CORNELL YEATS

PLAYS

The Countess Cathleen, edited by Michael J. Sidnell and Wayne K. Chapman
The Land of Heart's Desire, edited by Jared Curtis
Diarmuid and Grania, edited by J. C. C. Mays
Collaborative One-Act Plays, 1901–1903, "Cathleen ni Houlihan," "The Pot of Broth," "The Country of the Young," "Heads or Harps," by W. B. Yeats and Lady Gregory, edited by James Pethica
The Hour-Glass, edited by Catherine Phillips
The King's Threshold, edited by Declan Kiely
Deirdre, edited by Virginia Bartholome Rohan
"The Golden Helmet" and "The Green Helmet," edited by William P. Hogan
"The Dreaming of the Bones" and "Calvary," edited by Wayne K. Chapman
Sophocles' Oedipus at Colonus, edited by Jared Curtis
"The Only Jealousy of Emer" and "Fighting the Waves," edited by Steven Winnett
The Words Upon the Window Pane, edited by Mary FitzGerald
"The King of the Great Clock Tower" and "A Full Moon in March," edited by Richard Allen Cave
The Herne's Egg, edited by Alison Armstrong
Purgatory, edited by Sandra F. Siegel
The Death of Cuchulain, edited by Phillip L. Marcus

POEMS

The Early Poetry, Volume I: "Mosada" and "The Island of Statues," edited by George Bornstein
The Early Poetry, Volume II: "The Wanderings of Oisin" and Other Early Poems to 1895, edited by George Bornstein
The Wind Among the Reeds, edited by Carolyn Holdsworth
"In the Seven Woods" and "The Green Helmet and Other Poems," edited by David Holdeman
Responsibilities, edited by William H. O'Donnell
The Wild Swans at Coole, edited by Stephen Parrish
Michael Robartes and the Dancer, edited by Thomas Parkinson, with Anne Brannen
The Tower (1928), edited by Richard J. Finneran, with assistance from Jared Curtis and Ann Saddlemyer
The Winding Stair (1929), edited by David R. Clark
Words for Music, Perhaps, edited by David R. Clark
"Parnell's Funeral and Other Poems" from "A Full Moon in March," edited by David R. Clark
New Poems, edited by J. C. C. Mays and Stephen Parrish
Last Poems, edited by James Pethica

"The Golden Helmet" and "The Green Helmet"

Manuscript Materials

BY W. B. YEATS

EDITED BY

WILLIAM P. HOGAN

Cornell University Press

ITHACA AND LONDON

This book has been published with the aid of a grant from the
Hull Memorial Publication Fund of Cornell University.

First published 2009 by Cornell University Press

Printed in the United States of America

Library of Congress Cataloging-in-Publication Data

Yeats, W. B. (William Butler), 1865-1939.
[Golden helmet]
The golden helmet ; and, The green helmet : manuscript materials / by W.B. Yeats ; edited by William Hogan.
p. cm. -- (The Cornell Yeats)
ISBN 978-0-8014-4704-4 (cloth : alk. paper)
1. Yeats, W. B. (William Butler), 1865-1939. Golden helmet--Criticism, Textual. 2. Yeats, W. B. (William Butler), 1865-1939. Green helmet--Criticism, Textual. 3. Yeats, W. B. (William Butler), 1865-1939--Manuscripts--Facsimiles. I. Hogan, William (William P.) II. Yeats, W. B. (William Butler), 1865-1939. Green helmet. III. Title. IV. Title: Green helmet. V. Series: Yeats, W. B. (William Butler), 1865-1939. Works. 1982.

PR5904.G5 2009
821'.8--dc22

2009010910

Cornell University strives to utilize environmentally responsible suppliers and materials to the fullest extent possible in the publishing of its books. Such materials include vegetable-based, low-VOC inks and acid-free papers that are recycled, totally chlorine-free, or partly composed of non-wood fibers. For further information, visit our website at www.cornellpress.cornell.edu.

1 3 5 7 9 cloth printing 10 8 6 4 2

The Cornell Yeats

The volumes in this series present all available manuscripts, revised typescripts, proof-sheets, and other materials that record the growth of Yeats's poems and plays from the earliest draftings through to the texts published in his lifetime. Most of the materials are from the archives of the late Senator Michael Yeats, now in the care of the National Library of Ireland, supplemented by materials held by the late Anne Yeats; the remainder are preserved in public collections and private hands in Ireland and around the world. The volumes of poems, with a few exceptions, follow the titles of Yeats's own collections; several volumes of plays in the series contain more than one play.

In all the volumes manuscripts are reproduced in photographs accompanied by transcriptions, in order to illuminate Yeats's creative process—to show the poet at work. The remaining materials—such as clean typescripts and printed versions—are generally recorded in collated form in an apparatus hung below a finished text. Each volume contains an Introduction describing the significance of the materials it includes, tracing the relation of the various texts to one another. There is also a census of manuscripts, with full descriptive detail, and appendixes are frequently used to present related materials, some of them unpublished.

As the editions seek to present, comprehensively and accurately, the various versions behind Yeats's published poems and plays, including versions he left unpublished, they will be of use to readers who seek to understand how great writing can take shape, and to scholars and editors who seek to establish and verify authoritative final texts.

The Yeats Editorial Board

To the memory of Kevin M. O'Neill

Contents

Acknowledgments

This volume, as with all volumes in this series, is made possible by the generosity of the Yeats family, especially Gráinne Yeats and the late Anne Yeats and Michael B. Yeats, who provided open access to the materials here and gave permission to publish them.

The community of scholars associated with the Cornell Yeats series have astonished me, not only with their knowledge and expertise, but with their untiring willingness to help, encourage, and guide me in this project. I am grateful to the members of the editorial board of the series: to J. C. C. Mays, who welcomed me cheerfully from the moment I was appointed editor of this volume and provided invaluable help at the National Library of Ireland; to Declan Kiely, who helped me with questions about the New York Public Library; to Ann Saddlemyer; and especially to Jared Curtis, who provided research advice, meticulous editorial assistance, and with his wife, Ida, twice welcomed my family into his home on the beach in Connecticut. Other editors in the series have helpfully responded to my questions as well, especially James Pethica, David Holdeman, Catherine Phillips, and Wim van Mierlo.

I am grateful to the following institutions for permission to quote or reproduce materials from their collections: the Council of Trustees of the National Library of Ireland; the John Quinn Memorial Collection, Manuscripts and Archives Division, New York Public Library; the Manuscript Collections of the British Library.

A project like this is impossible without frequent assistance from the librarians and staff members at the various archives that house Yeats's manuscript materials. In particular, I am grateful to Catherine Fahy and Tom Desmond at the National Library of Ireland; Kristen Nyitray at Special Collections and Archives, the Frank Melville Jr. Library, State University of New York at Stony Brook; Isaac Gewirtz and Stephen Crook at the Henry W. and Albert A. Berg Collection of the New York Public Library; Richard Clement and Karen Severud Cook at the Kenneth Spencer Research Library, University of Kansas; Kathy Shoemaker of Special Collections, the Robert W. Woodruff Library, Emory University; Caitlin Murray at the Harry Ransom Humanities Research Center, University of Texas at Austin. I am grateful to the staff at Phillips Memorial Library, Providence College, who helped with requests of all kinds, ranging from arranging interlibrary loans to providing patient computer consultation. My work on this volume was also generously assisted by a grant from the Committee on Aid to Faculty Research at Providence College.

I am grateful, as ever, to George Bornstein for his unfailing generosity with advice and encouragement. I have been lucky to have his wise counsel through this and many other research projects.

Other colleagues at institutions around the world also helped with advice, commentary on early drafts of the project, and general good fellowship in conversations about this edition. I want to acknowledge, especially, all of my colleagues at Providence College, both in the English department and outside of it. One could not ask for a more hospitable and friendly place to work.

Kristina Reardon provided research assistance of all kinds, from helping with transcriptions to tracking down early reviews of the *Helmet* in performance. The project would have suffered greatly without her help.

And finally, love and thanks to my family, Erin, Andrew, and Will, who tolerated me while I buried the house under photocopies and scribbled scraps of paper.

WILLIAM P. HOGAN

Providence College

Abbreviations

BL	British Library
CL4	*The Collected Letters of W. B. Yeats,* vol. 4, *1905–1907*, ed. John Kelly and Ronald Suchard (Oxford: Clarendon Press, 2005).
CL Archive	*The Collected Letters of W. B. Yeats* (Oxford University Press InteLex Electronic Edition, 2002). The digital archive of letters by W. B. Yeats remaining to be published in *The Collected Letters of W. B. Yeats*, ed. John Kelly (Oxford University Press). Cited by accession number.
CPl	*Collected Plays* (London: Macmillan, 1934; Wade 177).
Cuala	*The Green Helmet and Other Poems* (Dundrum: Cuala Press, 1910; Wade 84).
EdL	The unpublished Edition de Luxe of the works of W. B. Yeats.
Foster 1	R. F. Foster, *W. B. Yeats: A Life,* vol. 1, *The Apprentice Mage, 1865–1914* (Oxford: Oxford University Press, 1997).
Foster 2	R. F. Foster, *W. B. Yeats: A Life,* vol. 2, *The Arch-Poet, 1915–1939* (Oxford: Oxford University Press, 2003).
GY	George Yeats (Mrs. W. B. Yeats)
L	*The Letters of W. B. Yeats*, ed. Allan Wade (New York: Macmillan, 1955).
LG	Lady Augusta Gregory
MS, MSS	Manuscript, manuscripts
NLI	National Library of Ireland
NYPL	New York Public Library
O'Shea	Edward O'Shea, *A Descriptive Catalog of W. B. Yeats's Library* (New York: Garland, 1985). Cited by item number.
TM	Thomas Mark, editor at Macmillan Publishers in London
TS, TSS	Typescript, typescripts
VPl	W. B. Yeats, *The Variorum Edition of the Plays of W. B. Yeats*, ed. Russell K. Alspach (London: Macmillan, 1966).
Wade	Allan Wade, *A Bibliography of the Writings of W. B. Yeats*, 3d ed. rev. and ed. Russell K. Alspach (London: Rupert Hart-Davis, 1968). Cited by item number.
WBY	William Butler Yeats

Census of Manuscripts

Measurements are recorded throughout in centimeters, width followed by height.

BL(1) A set of page proofs of EdL. Date stamped between October 9, 1937, and February 8, 1939, and marked up with corrections in the hands of TM and GY. Add. MS 55884, Macmillan Archive, BL.

BL(2) A set of page proofs for *CPl*. Date stamped with various dates between July 5, 1934, and August 9, 1934, and marked up with corrections in the hands of WBY and TM, including substantive revisions to *The Green Helmet*. The title page is stamped "First Proof," and TM has written "Revise to / T. Mark / c/o M & Co." and "Author's marked / proofs." Add. MS 55879, Macmillan Archive, BL.

NLI 1,731 A scrapbook of clippings related to the Abbey Theatre company during the years 1907–1909, including cast photographs, newspaper and magazine reviews, Abbey Theatre correspondence, and performance programs. The scrapbook is held in the W. A. Henderson collection, NLI. Two cast photographs for *The Golden Helmet*'s first production, in March 1908, are on pp. 34 and 37 of the scrapbook. See Appendix B, below, for the photographs.

NLI 8,761 A thirty-eight-page holograph fair copy of *The Green Helmet*, in WBY's hand, dating from late 1909 or early 1910. Written in black ink on cream-colored ruled paper removed from an exercise book, approximately 16.7 cm by 23 cm. On pp. 6^v, 21^v, 25^v, and 26^v are draft fragments of the material appearing on the corresponding recto.

NLI 13,571 An envelope containing a nineteen-page typescript of WBY's notes for his plays, marked with minor revisions in black ink, probably by WBY. On buff typing paper without watermark, approximately 20.3 cm by 25.4 cm. Prepared circa 1933 for EdL. Some of the notes are typed, some are cut from a print copy of *Plays in Prose and Verse* (London: Macmillan, 1922) and pasted on to the page. The note for *The Green Helmet* appears on typescript p. 16; it has been cut and pasted from *Plays in Prose and Verse* and has not been marked for revision.

NLI 21,503 An undated carbon-copy typescript prompt-copy of *The Green Helmet*, from the Abbey Theatre collection at NLI. Conall's lines are underlined in black pencil. This typescript incorporates textual changes dating from the 1934 Macmillan *CPl*.

NLI 29,548/1 A copy of the theater edition of *The Green Helmet: An Heroic Farce* (Stratford: Shakespeare Head Press, 1911).

NLI 29,548/2 and 3 A set of carbon copy typescript prompt-copies of *The Green Helmet*.

NLI 30,006/4 One gathering of a set of page proofs for vol. 3 (the first of two volumes of WBY's plays) of EdL. This gathering of proofs is date stamped November 19, 1931. *The Green Helmet* was originally to be the last play in vol. 3 of EdL; however, on the title page of *The Green Helmet* in these proofs is the note "This begins new / Vol. IV" by TM. *The Green Helmet* is marked with setting revisions by TM and possibly by others, but not by WBY. Among those revisions noted in TM's hand are substantive revisions to the play made by WBY and dating from 1934, so this set of proofs must have been corrected several years after they were printed.

NYPL A galley proof of the American edition of *The Golden Helmet* (New York: John Quinn, 1908). Minor copy edits marked in black ink, possibly by WBY. John Quinn Memorial Collections, Division of Rare Books and Manuscripts, NYPL.

YL(1) A copy of *The Golden Helmet* (New York: John Quinn, 1908; O'Shea 2352a; Wade 74), marked in blue ink and black pencil in an unidentified hand, not by WBY. Numbered copy 22 of 50.

YL(2) A copy of vol. 4 of *Collected Works in Verse and Prose* (Stratford: Shakespeare Head Press, 1908; O'Shea 2328; Wade 78).

YL(3) A copy of *Plays for an Irish Theatre* (London: A. H. Bullen, 1911; O'Shea 2397a; Wade 92).

Introduction

On March 30, 1908, Yeats wrote to his American friend and benefactor John Quinn to ask him to arrange for a small New York publication of Yeats's new play *The Golden Helmet*, in order to secure the American copyright. "I send you a proof of a dramatic trifle of mine," Yeats wrote, "which has no existence off the stage. . . . We produced it on March 19 & the next two nights & repeat it next week. It was finely played. It is a bubble blown in three days but it serves its purpose."[1] Judging from Yeats's other correspondence, his suggestion that he wrote the play over three days may be only a slight exaggeration; it was certainly composed at great speed, especially for a writer as meticulous and prone to revision as Yeats was.

Yet this "bubble" of a play, later revised into verse and retitled *The Green Helmet*, was also cited by Padraic Colum as Yeats's "most effective play," and Yeats himself retained a long-standing affection for its "animated gay effective stage not too far from the mood of the world."[2] And it is certainly the case that the *Helmet* plays, written between July 1907 and February 1910, occupied Yeats's creative energies during a crucial period of transition in his artistic, political, and personal development. During this time, Yeats began to shift his focus away from full-time work at the Abbey Theatre and back to writing lyric poetry; his political ideas continued to shift away from more traditional forms of Irish nationalism; and Maud Gonne's divorce proceedings caused upheaval in his personal life. While the *Helmet* is a short one-act play and a comedy (which was not a natural mode for Yeats), it helps to illuminate this period in Yeats's work, when he was negotiating important tensions between theatrical work and verse writing; between national unity and individual genius; and between the life of the spirit and the sensations of the body. The *Helmet* play—which from the outset Yeats subtitled "an heroic farce"—is steeped in these tensions in both of its versions.

The *Helmet* plays return to source material drawn from Irish legend and filtered through Lady Gregory's 1902 collection of legends, *Cuchulain of Muirthemne*.[3] The story was meant as a companion piece to the earlier play *On Baile's Strand* ("which it prepares for," Yeats wrote to Quinn[4]) and forms part of Yeats's cycle of plays drawn from the life of the legendary Irish hero Cuchulain. Throughout his life, from *On Baile's Strand* in 1903 to *The Death of Cuchulain* in 1939, the character of Cuchulain provided Yeats with one of his favorite masks, allowing him to present different aspects of the hero's personality as his own interests and

---

[1]WBY to John Quinn, March 30, 1908, *CL* Archive, accession number 845.

[2]WBY to Allan Wade, October 18, 1921, *L*, p. 674. WBY quoted the remark made by Colum (1881–1972), an influential poet and playwright of Yeats's circle, in his letter to Wade.

[3]See Lady Gregory, *Cuchulain of Muirthemne: The Story of the Men of the Red Branch of Ulster* (London: J. Murray, 1902).

[4]WBY to John Quinn, March 30, 1908, *CL* Archive, accession number 845.

commitments changed.

But Yeats makes relatively free use of his source material, as was nearly always the case when he adapted classical and mythological subjects. The narrative of the *Helmet* conflates two legends from Lady Gregory's collection, "Bricriu's Feast" and "The Championship of Ulster." Three heroes of Ulster, Cuchulain, Conall, and Laegaire, gather to await the return from the sea of a mysterious Red Man. The Red Man had visited Conall and Laegaire one year previously, proposing a bloody game: in an echo of *Sir Gawain and the Green Knight*, the Red Man allows Conall to chop off his head on the condition that afterward Conall will allow the Red Man to respond in kind. When the Red Man returns, seeking to collect on this promise, he brings with him a magical helmet. He suggests that the three heroes contend for possession of the helmet; the winner will mark himself as the strongest warrior among them and the de facto leader of Ireland. Cuchulain wins the helmet, but he does so not through physical prowess but through clear judgment and selflessness. Against loud partisan clamoring, first from the heroes' servants and then from their wives, Cuchulain suggests wisely that the helmet is dividing the community. So, rather than allow any one faction to triumph, he throws the prize into the sea, despite fierce opposition from the other heroes, and even from his own wife, Emer. In the end, the Red Man returns, bringing the helmet, and he awards it to Cuchulain for his even-tempered and generous good nature. The Cuchulain of *The Helmet* stands in contrast with earlier heroes in Yeats's work, such as the Cuchulain of *On Baile's Strand*, whose tragic heroism derives more conventionally from physical prowess and uncontrollable passion. In the *Helmet*, Yeats associates the heroic with a noble capacity to stand apart from the clamoring crowd. The principle themes of the *Helmet* plays—the importance of iconoclasm, the shortcomings of public opinion, and the danger of groupthink—are bound up with this concept of the heroic.

The figure of the Red Man makes a useful example of Yeats's loose adaptation of his folkloric sources. Standing much taller than the other characters, dressed all in red, and crowned in the large horned helmet, he is perhaps the most visually striking presence in the play, as Yeats himself suggested after seeing the early performances.[5] And of course, in introducing the game of lopping off heads at a stroke, he is the source of the play's dramatic tension and also its prevailing mood of violent mischief. Yet in Lady Gregory's stories "Bricriu's Feast" and "The Championship of Ulster," there is no exact parallel for the Red Man. Rather, the figure seems to be a conflation of at least four characters from the two stories: the trickster figure Bricriu, who first instigates discord and competition among the Red Branch heroes; the civil authorities Maeve and Aillel, who try (but ultimately fail) to adjudicate the dispute; Uath, the Stranger, a mysterious figure who introduces the head-chopping game; and the wise magician Curoi, who had summoned Uath and ultimately pronounces Cuchulain the champion. It is not clear whether Yeats also had *Sir Gawain and the Green Knight* in mind when he was conceiving the *Helmet* plays, but in any case the legend of that poem, with its own head-cutting game, is parallel to the ones related in *Cuchulain at Muirthemne*. So the antecedents for the play establish its roots in both Celtic and English mythology, and they allow Yeats to trace his dramatic lineage to sources predating the Elizabethan drama, which had inspired his earlier thinking about the medium.

In its pulling together of several folkloric sources, the Red Man's narrative function in the play becomes quite complex, even fraught with competing impulses, and in this, he is a characteristically Yeatsian figure. At once, the character is a figure of violence and magic but also,

[5]In a letter to Quinn, Yeats wrote that the play in performance "makes a series of beautiful pictures & colours. The red man is a wonderful figure on the stage" (WBY to John Quinn, March 30, 1908, *CL* Archive, accession number 845).

in the end, one of law and justice. He is an important source of the play's farce, with his absurd demand for heads and his verbal abuse of the great Irish heroes. But he also proves deeply serious, especially at the play's conclusion, with his message celebrating Cuchulain—and of course Yeats was also thinking autobiographically here—for his "heart that grows no bitterer although betrayed by all."

Two major events in Yeats's life leading up to 1907 provide important context for the play and these thematic interests. First, in 1905, the Abbey Theatre was incorporated as a salaried company with Yeats, Lady Gregory, and J. M. Synge as its codirectors, and it lost some of its former identity as a kind of nationalist cooperative enterprise. Accordingly, tensions were exacerbated between Yeats, who was becoming more and more disillusioned with what he perceived to be the provincialism of popular forms of Irish nationalism, and some of his players, who liked the idea of the theater as a kind of revolutionary collective. This conflict between Yeats's vision for the theater and the ideas of some of its company and its core audience came famously to a head with the furor over the premiere of Synge's *Playboy of the Western World* in February 1907. Yeats's outrage over the Dublin audience's initial rejection of the play—and his distaste at the way the play was shouted down by an angry crowd—was surely fresh in his mind that July, when he wrote the earliest versions of the *Helmet*, with its heroic Cuchulain rising above such angry shouting.

Second, during April and May of 1907, just before he began the *Helmet*, he traveled to Italy with Lady Gregory and her son, Robert. In part, this was an attempt to escape the hostility Yeats felt in Dublin in the aftermath of the *Playboy* affair, but seeing Venice, Florence, and Ravenna for the first time only solidified his idealized notion of the culture of aristocratic patronage that he associated with the Italian Renaissance. As Foster puts it, "Castiglione, the 'grammar school of courtesies,' a life of artistic order and labour became central to his ideal."[6] The culture depicted in the *Helmet*—a kind of vibrant court presided over by the artist-hero Cuchulain, who swoops in from his retreat in "high windy Scotland" to resolve the crisis of the play—owes much to this new ideal.[7]

With these various developments in the background, Yeats wrote *The Golden Helmet* during the summer of 1907, and it was published twice during the following year: first in June, in the small American edition Yeats had requested from John Quinn; and then in October, in the sumptuous, eight-volume *Collected Works in Verse and Prose,* put out by A. H. Bullen's Shakespeare Head Press. Yeats rewrote the prose play into verse over the next two years, working sporadically. The verse version was first published in December 1910 as the title piece in the Cuala Press edition *The Green Helmet and Other Poems*. The text of the play remained stable for the next two decades, until it was slightly revised during the preparations of Macmillan's *Collected Plays* in 1934.

This edition presents the evolution of the *Helmet* plays through these three crucial moments: composition in prose and publication as *The Golden Helmet* in 1907–1908; revision into verse between 1908 and 1910, resulting in *The Green Helmet*; and finally, slight revision during the 1930s when *Collected Plays* was produced. The core of this evolution is an autograph manuscript of the initial verse revision (NLI 8761), dating from late 1909 or early 1910, in which we can see clearly the crucial moment of rethinking that accompanied transforming the play from a prose "trifle" into a more crafted play in verse.

---

[6]Foster 1, p. 369.

[7]The phrase appears in NLI 8761, 3^r, l. 2, below.

The Golden Helmet (1908) and *Collected Works in Verse and Prose* (1908)

In a letter to Lady Gregory on May 30, 1905, Yeats makes reference to an "expensive collected edition" of his works, apparently under discussion with A. H. Bullen, who had published several of Yeats's books since *The Secret Rose* in 1897. He writes that the collected edition would be postponed so that Bullen might bring out a collection of Yeats's recent poetry, a book that eventually became *Poems 1899–1905* (Wade 64).[8]

When Yeats returned to London in May of 1907 after his tour of Italy with the Gregorys, the plans for the collected edition had progressed, and financing for its production had been secured from the Abbey's (and Yeats's) patron Annie Horniman. After the stresses of the previous year, including the controversy over the *Playboy* premiere, as well as incessant infighting at the Abbey, Yeats felt powerfully as he returned from Italy that he had lost touch with his own writing. As he wrote to Lady Gregory at the end of June: "I feel that I have lost myself—my centre as it were, has shifted from its natural interests, and that it will take me a long time finding myself again."[9] Thus it must have been with some relief that he retired to Coole Park in July to spend the summer preparing his plays for *Collected Works in Verse and Prose* (1908).

Yet that work would soon be disrupted by Bullen's somewhat erratic business habits. Yeats was eager to proceed with his work for the proposed volumes in a systematic way: he assured Bullen that "[y]ou needn't have any anxiety about my text being ready for you, provided you always give me proper notice. I should know three weeks let us say beforehand when a new book is wanted."[10] But Bullen shocked Yeats by printing the volumes for the edition at a faster rate than he had anticipated, and Yeats found himself scrambling to write new material—including *The Golden Helmet*—for the volume of plays.

And it seems that he *did* scramble to write *The Golden Helmet*. On July 12, in a proposed table of contents for the edition that he sends to Bullen, Yeats reports that two new Cuchulain plays to be included in the edition are still to be written.[11] Just three weeks later, at the beginning of August, he writes that he has just completed *The Golden Helmet*, "except for verbal revision."[12] This rapid composition was hardly Yeats's customary way of working. Rather, he was much more likely to write and rewrite, revising and struggling over long periods to bring works into finished form.

There has been some question about whether the play that resulted from this accelerated production schedule was intended as a separate, finished play, or whether it is better classified as a prose scenario, a kind of narrative skeleton that could form the basis for subsequent polishing.[13] Certainly, Yeats was in the habit of sketching scenarios as a preliminary composition technique for both plays and for lyric poems. We have scenarios Yeats wrote for other plays from this general period, including *Deirdre* and *The Player Queen*. While *The Golden Helmet* resembles these other scenarios in some respects, it is the only one of them that Yeats published separately in its prose form. Whether Bullen's demand for copy played a role in that decision is not clear; but Yeats had ample opportunity to withdraw the play from *Collected Works in Verse and Prose*

---

[8] *L*, p. 449.

[9] WBY to LG, June 27, 1907, *CL4*, p. 681.

[10] WBY to A. H. Bullen, July 5, 1907, *CL4*, p. 689.

[11] One of these two plays was *The Golden Helmet*. See WBY to A. H. Bullen, July 12, 1907, *CL4*, p. 695.

[12] WBY to A. H. Bullen, August ?4, 1907, *CL4*, p. 704.

[13] One of the best considerations of this question, and of the other issues involved in the evolution of the *Helmet* from conception through its prose and verse versions remains S. B. Bushrui, *Yeats's Verse Plays: The Revisions, 1900–1910* (Oxford: Clarendon Press, 1965), especially pp. 168–208.

before the edition was completed, and he chose to go ahead with publication.

But regardless of whether *The Golden Helmet* was intended as a scenario or a finished play, in a number of ways it represented a new direction in Yeats's work for the theater. Most notably, it shows him experimenting for the first time with comedic and satiric modes for treating the mythic and heroic materials that had been attracting his imagination for years. In R. F. Foster's phrase, "dreamy Celticism was dissolving behind him";[14] in its place, Yeats was increasingly attracted to the mythic tableaux of the Elizabethan stage: chaotic, vibrant, funny, "rammed with life," as Yeats later put it.[15] He had spent the summer of 1906 in a close study of Dekker and Jonson, and one can see some of these influences in the comic mode of *The Golden Helmet*. The stage is frequently occupied by clamoring crowds, and in the midst of this bustle rise stylized, larger-than-life heroes like Cuchulain and the tall, mysterious Red Man.

In addition to revealing the influence of Yeats's studies in satiric drama and the Jonsonian masque, *The Golden Helmet* also provided Yeats with a vehicle for some of his new ideas about the visual spectacle of the drama. Throughout his time at the Abbey, Yeats expended a good deal of energy and time imagining the theatrical aspects of his plays—the lighting, the costumes, the manner of the actors' speech—in addition to the words in the text. By 1907, however, and in particular in *The Golden Helmet*, Yeats was experimenting with new kinds of visual spectacle. The staging for the first *Helmet* production was highly stylized, rich in gesture and movement, and reflective of Yeats's developing interest in Japanese dramatic traditions. In a note to the text that appeared in the *Collected Works* edition[16] Yeats describes the visual effects he was imagining:

> We staged the play with a very pronounced colour-scheme, and I have noticed that the more obviously decorative is the scene and costuming of any play, the more it is lifted out of time and place, and the nearer to faeryland do we carry it. One gets also much more effect out of concerted movements—above all, if there are many players—when all the clothes are the same colour. No breadth of treatment gives monotony when there is movement and change of lighting. It concentrates attention on every new effect and makes every change of outline or of light and shadow surprising and delightful. Because of this one can use contrasts of colour, between clothes and background or in the background itself, the complementary colours for instance, which would be too obvious to keep the attention in a painting.

Thus we see how much of Yeats's conception of this work had to do with its visual aspect; accounts of the early productions dwell on the rich and eerie contrast of red and black in the costumes and lighting.

Some months passed between Yeats's August 4 announcement to Bullen that he had finished writing *The Golden Helmet* (except for "verbal revision") and his March 12, 1908, submission of the manuscript for typesetting. During that time, Yeats expressed reservations about the play's quality and appropriateness for publication on several occasions: on February 7, he told Bullen that he was "getting a little nervous about this play";[17] and on February 26, he wrote

---

[14]Foster 1, p. 345.

[15]See *Autobiographies* (London: Macmillan, 1955), p. 480.

[16]Included here in Appendix A.

[17]WBY to A. H. Bullen, February 7, 1908, *CL* Archive, accession number 776.

(after seeing *The Golden Helmet* in rehearsal) that it "may be good enough";[18] on the day of the play's opening, he wrote pessimistically to Lady Gregory that it "will suffer from imperfect rehersal [*sic*] of the extra people. . . . I am anxious about it."[19] Finally, just days before the play opened, he reported to Bullen that "I am at my wit's end about *Helmet*. My only copy, the prompt copy, has it seems been stolen from the theatre—at any rate it is lost. The actors will have to dictate the whole thing."[20] It was only after the actors had dictated the play back to Yeats, and on the eve of its opening performance, that he finally committed to including the play in Bullen's edition by submitting copy to the publisher on March 12.[21]

Despite these anxieties, the play proved to be successful in performance, both in Yeats's eyes and in the view of most reviewers. The day after opening night, only a day removed from his anxiety and pessimism, he wrote ebulliently that "'Golden Helmet' is a great success. Almost everybody seems agreed that it went the best of the three Plays last night. . . . The Scene was wonderful, the color extraordinarily striking, and the lighting very picturesque. Power made a magnificent figure with something supernatural about him in the dim light, a real Mananan [*sic*] son of the sea at last."[22] If he had doubts about including the play in *Collected Works,* it seems that the success of the play in performance eased his fears.

Ultimately, the play appeared in volume four of Bullen's edition, along with *The Hour-Glass, Cathleen ni Houlihan,* and a collection of Yeats's prose writing about drama and the theater that was gathered as *The Irish Dramatic Movement*. All eight volumes of Bullen's edition appeared in the last half of 1908, and volume four itself was published in October. The print run for the collected edition was 1,060 sets, and both Yeats himself and the reviewers of the edition seem to have agreed that the books were beautifully made.[23] However, despite their beauty, despite Annie Horniman's financial subsidy of the edition, and despite the fact that the edition sold rather well, it proved to be a financial disaster for Bullen: in 1919, more than ten years later, he still owed Yeats thirty pounds.[24]

Meanwhile, a few months before the Shakespeare Head edition appeared, John Quinn had complied with Yeats's request to produce a small American edition in order to protect copyright. In June 1908, Quinn's privately published edition appeared in a print run of fifty copies. Therefore, though Bullen's *Collected Works* was the first commercial edition of the play, Quinn's small edition represents the first publication of *The Golden Helmet*. Indeed, after all of the negotiating with Bullen over the Shakespeare Head edition, no autograph manuscript or even corrected proof from that edition survives. As a result, the transcription I have included in the present edition is of a galley proof for the John Quinn edition in New York, a proof that Yeats read but did not revise.

---

[18]WBY to A. H. Bullen, February 26, 1908, *CL* Archive, accession number 795.

[19]WBY to LG, March 19, 1908, *CL* Archive, accession number 834.

[20]WBY to A. H. Bullen, March 1908, *L,* p. 505.

[21]WBY to A. H. Bullen, March 12, 1908, *CL* Archive, accession number 828.

[22]WBY to LG, March 20, 1908, *CL* Archive, accession number 835. Ambrose Power played the role of the Red Man in the first production of *The Golden Helmet* on March 19, 1908.

[23]At the end of April 1908, WBY wrote to John Quinn that "this collected edition is going to be a beautiful thing. I have seen the first specimen volume and am well content with my share of it and with Bullen's. I think I am better in the mass than in fragments." *L*, p. 509.

[24]For an account of the Shakespeare Head Press, and of Bullen's financial difficulties, see Frank Sidgwick's *Diary and Other Material Relating to A. H. Bullen and the Shakespeare Head Press* (Oxford: Shakespeare Head Press, 1975).

The Green Helmet: NLI 8761 and *The Green Helmet and Other Poems* (1910)

If *The Golden Helmet* was, for Yeats, a work that had "no existence apart from the stage," *The Green Helmet* was much more a poetic and textual artifact. After meticulously rewriting the *Helmet* story into loosely rhymed fourteen-beat lines, or fourteeners, between 1908 and 1910, Yeats was initially dismayed at how the new version translated onto the stage. After seeing a performance in May 1910, a few months after it had opened, Yeats wrote to Lady Gregory that "I thought the Green Helmet show so bad that I would like to strike it out of the London bill. . . . I don't think Robinson understands verse work or feels the importance of little things in verse."[25] As he repeated on many other occasions, Yeats felt that for verse plays, the poetic language must be paramount—everything else about the performance was secondary to the skillful speaking of the verse.

The difference between his reaction to *The Green Helmet* and his much more enthusiastic response to performances of *The Golden Helmet* is instructive: as Yeats labored for two years over the verse revision, the *Helmet* became less of a theatrical spectacle and more of a long poem, carefully crafted and intended as much for the page as for the stage. This transition is visible in the manuscript record, as we can see more of Yeats's characteristic meticulousness as he worked and reworked the play.

As soon as—and quite possibly before—*The Golden Helmet* was in print, Yeats began his verse revision. *The Golden Helmet* appeared in Bullen's *Collected Works* edition in October of 1908. On the seventeenth of that month, Yeats reported in a letter to Lady Gregory that he had been reworking the play but was having trouble finding time to work on it.[26] This pattern would continue over the next two years: in his correspondence, Yeats periodically reports working on the revision amid his other projects and obligations. Indeed, it seems that the *Helmet* revision served as a kind of relaxation and a way to recondition himself after nearly a decade away from serious verse-writing. "I am inclined to try a couple of lines a day at 'Golden Helmet,'" he wrote in March of 1909, "& am getting Morris's 'Seugurd the Volsung' which is in the same metre as it will give me every variety of line so that I can judge the effect of various treatments."[27] A few days later, he reports feeling under the weather but writes that "if I could have had a hours work on 'Golden Helmet' I believe it would have made me quite well again—I need a little verse writing every day I believe to keep in health absurd as it sounds."[28]

For the revision, Yeats chose a long metrical line, the fourteener. In his earlier verse plays, Yeats had typically used blank verse, under the influence of the drama of the English Renaissance. But he had admired the longer line in Wilfrid Scawen Blunt's *Fand of the Fair Cheek*, which had played at the Abbey in 1904, and wanted to experiment with it for his heroic plays. As he would explain later in his "General Introduction for My Work," "our Heroic Age went better, or so I fancied, in the ballad metre of *The Green Helmet*. There was something about

[25]WBY to LG, May 23, 1910, *CL* Archive, accession number 1361. Lennox Robinson (1886–1958) had become manager of the Abbey at the end of 1909.

[26]WBY to LG, October 17, 1908, *CL* Archive, accession number 975.

[27]WBY to LG, March 4, 1909, *CL* Archive, accession number 1102. William Morris (1834–1896) was an English poet, designer, and artist, and an important influence on WBY. Morris translated Norse sagas into English verse, and some of these were published as *The Story of Sigurd the Volsung and the Fall of the Niblung* (1876).

[28]WBY to LG, March 11, 1909, *CL* Archive, accession number 1110.

Deirdre, about Cuchulain, that rejected the Renaissance and its characteric metres."[29] So, during 1908 and 1909, Yeats worked at translating the narrative of *The Golden Helmet* into this new meter, and by December 22, 1909, he reported to Lady Gregory that "in about three days I shall have come to the end of Golden Helmet. I shall still have to copy it out making small revisions but it will be ready for early performance."[30]

As it happened, he continued to work with the play over the next weeks, alternately reporting that he had "quite finished with it" and that he finds "a lot of little things to alter."[31] The ending of the play was the last portion to be completed to his satisfaction: on January 8, 1910, he wrote that he has improved Emer's song from the last pages of the manuscript, and in a letter to Lady Gregory dated February 11, 1910, the morning after the premiere of *The Green Helmet* at the Abbey, he copied out the play's final speech.[32] Interestingly, one of the last things to be changed seems to have been the title of the play. On January 8, he still refers to it as *The Golden Helmet*; by opening night, on February 10, it had become *The Green Helmet*. In the autograph manuscript that survives in the National Library of Ireland, and is reproduced and transcribed in this edition, the play is titled simply *The Helmet*.

That manuscript (NLI 8761) is undated, but it probably was written during the weeks between December 22, 1909, and January 8, 1910. It is clearly a very late draft of the play—with a few exceptions, the text is the one that was eventually published by the Cuala Press in *Green Helmet and Other Poems* in December 1910. The last lines of the play are not yet in their final form, and Emer's song shows signs of writing and rewriting. Much of the rest of the manuscript is a relatively clean copy that is consistent with Yeats's reports in his correspondence of repeatedly "finishing" the play, copying it out, and then continuing to struggle with it.

By revising *The Golden Helmet* into the verse of *The Green Helmet* Yeats added vitality to the narrative.[33] Yet reading the two texts side by side reveals that he kept quite close to the original version, essentially translating events, speeches, and even most of the images and figures of language from prose into verse. In both versions, the central images of cats, the helmet, and the phantoms from under the sea remain the same, and the eerie lighting and stark color scheme seem to have been a crucial component in the performance of both plays.

Though in most respects Yeats hewed fairly closely to the prose version as he reworked it into verse, the major exception to this comes at the end of the play in the treatment of the relationship between Cuchulain and Emer. At the conclusion of both plays, when Cuchulain offers to give up his head in order to pay the Red Man's rightful debt, Emer objects, urging Cuchulain to reconsider. But in *The Golden Helmet*, Emer is not a particularly central figure. She merely wails when Cuchulain offers himself up, and Cuchulain dismisses her objection, arguing that his passionate nature compels him to make this sacrifice, and that she should not try to change him:

---

[29]See W. B. Yeats, *Later Essays*, ed. William H. O'Donnell (New York: Charles Scribner's Sons, 1994), p. 214. In its published versions, *The Green Helmet* does not exhibit the characteristic split lines of ballad meter; but in the manuscript reproduced and transcribed here, Yeats frequently splits the lines with a comma or other mark, suggesting that he was thinking in lines of two balanced halves, as in ballad meter.

[30]WBY to LG, December 22, 1909, *CL* Archive, accession number 1249.

[31]See WBY to LG, January 8, 1910, and February 11, 1910, *CL* Archive, accession numbers 1262 and 1296.

[32]Ibid.

[33]He seems to have agreed that this was the case, writing Lady Gregory near the end of the revision that she "will like 'Golden Helmet' now. It has got some passion [in] it at last." See WBY to LG, January 8, 1910, *CL* Archive, accession number 1262.

Do not cry out, Emer,
for if I were not myself, if I were not Cuchulain,
one of those that God has made reckless, the
women of Ireland had not loved me, and you
had not held your head so high. (NYPL, ll. 402–406)[34]

Emer has no response to this argument in *The Golden Helmet*, and after this brief exchange, we do not hear from her again in the play.

In *The Green Helmet*, however, Emer becomes a much more prominent presence. Cuchulain argues that his martyrdom will only increase Emer's honor among the people, and Emer responds, sensibly: "It is you not your fame that I love." When Cuchulain suggests that he cannot be dissuaded from his decision to sacrifice himself, Emer draws her own dagger and tries to commit suicide rather than helplessly watch Cuchulain die. In essence, Emer becomes a partner to Cuchulain's sacrifice, and in *The Green Helmet*, the two become a kind of balanced pairing, in which each is dependent on, and strengthened by, the other. This is an idea that comes through strongly in the lyric that Emer sings at the conclusion of *The Green Helmet*:

Nothing that he has done,
His mind that is fire,
His body that is sun,
Have set my head higher,
Than all the world's wives.
Himself on the wind
Is the gift that he gives,
Therefore women kind,
When their eyes have met mine,
Grow cold and grow hot
Troubled as with wine
By a secret thought,
Preyed upon, fed upon
By jealousy and desire,
For I am moon to that sun,
I am steel to that fire[35]

The lyric, full of mutually reinforcing opposites (mind/body; moon/sun; cold/hot; steel/fire) figures Emer not merely as Cuchulain's equal but as his complement, the source of an opposing energy that completes and strengthens Cuchulain.

This idea, of energies bound to one another, often through violence, had long been part of Yeats's imagination. But placed in the context of the relationship between Cuchulain and Emer, one thinks naturally of Yeats's intense ongoing relationship with Maud Gonne. At the end of 1909, when the final version of Emer's lyric was taking shape, Yeats had recently renewed his close contact with Gonne. After her divorce proceedings from John MacBride had been concluded in 1906, Gonne had been with Yeats in London in the summer of 1909. He became convinced again that he was bound to her in spiritual marriage. This idea of a mystical bonding that

[34]See p. 15, below.

[35]W. B. Yeats, *The Green Helmet and Other Poems* (Dundrum: Cuala Press, 1910), pp. 28–29.

transcends any physical connection illuminates the new intensity of the relationship between Cuchulain and Emer in the revised *Helmet*.

In NLI 8761, the manuscript of *The Green Helmet* reproduced and transcribed here, we get a clear picture of Emer's song taking shape, and with it, Emer's more powerful presence in the play. We know that Yeats worked on the Emer lyric on January 8, 1910, when he wrote to Lady Gregory: "I am still heavy with influenza but getting better as I know from having improved a lyric in 'Golden Helmet' this morning. Emer's song which is now quite good."[36] The manuscript NLI 8761, though it is undated, shows heavy revision to the lyric, and it seems probable that it is the manuscript he mentions in the letter.

Indeed, the changes he made significantly improve the lyric, streamlining the verse and strengthening the theme of opposing energies that is so central to the end of the play in its final form. In *The Golden Helmet*, each of the heroes' wives sings a song of praise for her husband. Laegaire's wife and Conal's wife are each given ten lines of verse, while Emer is given sixteen. Yet in this first form, Emer's song is quite pedestrian. It is straightforward in its praise of Cuchulain and emphasizes that all of Ireland's women envy Emer because she has been "young and handsome" enough to win them over:

> My man is the best
> And Conal's wife
> And the wife of Leagerie
> Know that they lie
> When they praise their own
> Out of envy of me.

In contrast to the final form of the song, in this early version there is no mention of Emer's terrible power and violent energy, traits that complement Cuchulain's level-headedness and stoicism at this moment in the play.

When one examines the revisions to the song visible in NLI 8761, and the further revisions that must have followed before *The Green Helmet's* first publication, one sees Yeats working steadily toward this new conception of Emer as the terrible complement to Cuchulain.[37] First, he collapses the other heroes' wives two songs into one, given to Laegaire's wife; this makes Emer's song more prominent and striking. Then, he seems to have extended Emer's song significantly, giving her, at first, over thirty lines of verse. In the manuscript, he writes these lines on a single side of an exercise book page, dividing the lyric into two columns (see pp. 84–85, below).

The first column of the song is quite similar in theme and content to the earlier version in *The Golden Helmet*: Emer sings of other women's envy of her, and she boasts of her "prouder eye / And younger face." In the second column, however, the lyric sharpens its focus when Yeats hits upon some of the central images of the song's final version, including the oppositions like body/ mind, cold/hot, and steel/fire. It seems probable that these final lines were the last to develop, because the verso notebook page (see pp. 82–83, below) shows him working out the end of the song in a rapid pencil scribble. As is frequently visible in his revisions, this rapid, late burst of inspiration leads him to definite improvements in both rhythm and diction. For example, "His body is a sun / His mind is a fire / That not what he's done / Has set my head higher / That all

[36]WBY to LG, January 8, 1910, *CL* Archive, accession number 1262.

[37]For the following discussion, see Part II, pp. 77–89, below.

the world's wives" becomes "Nothing that he has done / His mind that is fire / His body that is sun / Has set my head higher / Than all the world's wives."

Along with these improvements, he shortened the lyric significantly, cutting the first half, which had contained the ideas and images from *The Golden Helmet*. While he does not cancel the first half of the lyric in NLI 8761, he did so before *The Green Helmet* was published at the end of the year, ultimately reducing the song's length to the sixteen lines it had occupied in *The Golden Helmet*.

The Green Helmet, in its revised version, was first published by the Cuala Press as the concluding piece in *The Green Helmet and Other Poems* (1910). The central themes of the lyrics in that volume—for example, Yeats's spiritual connection to Maud Gonne ("No Second Troy") and his lament over Irish popular opinion ("Upon a Threatened House"; "King and No King")—resonate powerfully with the play that served as its anchor. These resonances were made even stronger in the 1912 Macmillan version of *The Green Helmet and Other Poems*. While the text of the play is identical in both versions of the collection, Yeats added six new poems to the 1912 edition, many of which closely inform the themes of the play.[38]

Collected Plays (1934) and the Edition de Luxe

After Yeats completed the revisions for the publication of *The Green Helmet and Other Poems*, the text of the play remained the same for two decades, until Yeats revisited it during the preparations for the Macmillan *Collected Plays* (1934). At that time, Yeats made one substantive change to the text. The manuscripts involved in that revision are reproduced and transcribed in the second part of this edition; they are BL(2), the corrected proofs for *Collected Plays*, and BL(1) and NLI 30,006, which are proofs for the never-published Macmillan Edition de Luxe. The sequence of events surrounding the revisions Yeats made to *The Green Helmet* in the 1930s are complex and bound up with the story of the Edition de Luxe, and so they bear some explanation.[39]

Yeats signed and returned a contract for the publication of a multivolume collector's edition of his complete works on May 4, 1931.[40] At that time, the plays were projected to be included in volumes 3 and 4 of the new edition. Proofs for these volumes were printed and date-stamped in 1931 and are now held in the Yeats archive at the National Library of Ireland.[41] Though Yeats read and corrected some of the proofs for the Edition de Luxe that were printed in 1931, it does not appear that he read the ones for *The Green Helmet*. The ambitious edition was delayed by poor economic conditions in the early 1930s, and it seems that the 1931 proofs of volume 3, which contain *The Green Helmet*, were stored unread.

---

38 Among the new poems in this edition (Wade 101) were "The Cold Heaven," "On Those That Hated *The Playboy of the Western World*," and "At the Abbey Theatre." For more discussion of the differences between the 1910 and 1912 *Green Helmet and Other Poems*, see David Holdeman, ed., *"In the Seven Woods" and "The Green Helmet and Other Poems": Manuscript Materials* (Ithaca: Cornell University Press, 2002).

39 A full reporting of the complicated story of the Edition de Luxe has been ably made by several scholars. The most complete accounts are contained in Warwick Gould, Philip Marcus, and Michael J. Sidnell, *The Secret Rose, Stories by W. B. Yeats: A Variorum Edition* (Ithaca: Cornell University Press, 1981), especially pp. xvii–xxxiv; Richard J. Finneran, *Editing Yeats's Poems* (London: Macmillan, 1983); and Foster 2, pp. 415–417, 434, 460–461, 534, 653–654. Both the *Secret Rose* edition and Finneran's *Editing Yeats's Poems* were published in second editions that further illuminated the publication history of the Edition de Luxe. See *Editing Yeats's Poems* (New York: St. Martin's, 1991) and *The Secret Rose* (London: MacMillan, 1992).

40 See A. P. Watt & Son to Macmillan & Co., May 4, 1931, *CL* Archive, accession number 5464.

41 See NLI 30,006/4, below.

By 1933, no progress had been made toward publishing the Edition de Luxe. Yeats had new work that he wanted to publish and, quite simply, he needed income, and so, given the delays with the de Luxe, Macmillan agreed in 1933 to produce a single-volume *Collected Poems* and a book of new poems titled *The Winding Stair*. These volumes were both commercially successful, and so the publisher agreed to follow them up with a single-volume *Collected Plays* in 1934. While the earlier proofs for the Edition de Luxe remained uncorrected, Yeats revised the proofs for the single-volume *Collected Plays* in 1934, and the book was published that same year.

On the *Collected Plays* proofs, Yeats made substantive changes to a passage late in the play in which Emer and the other heroes' wives enter to support their husbands' claims to the helmet. In earlier versions of the play, Cuchulain orders the windows of the house to be widened into doors so that all three women might enter at the same time: "Break down the painted boards between the sill and the floor / That they come in together, each one at her own door."[42] In the 1934 revision, Yeats changes the lines to read "Break down the painted walls, break them down, down to the floor / Our wives shall come in together, each one at her own door."[43] This is a minor change, to be sure, but it represents the only moment in the play that Yeats revised during the 1930s. This revised reading has generally been preferred in subsequent printings of the plays, including in the current standard edition, David R. Clark and Rosalind E. Clark's volume of *Plays* for the Scribner *Collected Works of W. B. Yeats* (New York: Scribner, 2001).

The markings on the three manuscripts from the 1930s suggest that after Yeats corrected the proofs for *Collected Plays* in 1934, the 1931 Edition de Luxe proofs were revisited by Thomas Mark, a trusted editor of Yeats's at Macmillan. The revision Yeats made in 1934 to the entrance of the heroes' wives is copied back into the 1931 proofs in Mark's hand. The conjecture that the 1931 proofs were pulled out and corrected not before but *after* publication of the 1934 *Collected Plays* is consistent with the fact that the Edition de Luxe proofs were examined and marked up at several times during the 1930s, sometimes years after the proofs were originally printed. At some time during the 1930s, *The Green Helmet* was moved from its original place in volume 3 of the Edition de Luxe to the beginning of volume 4; this change is marked on the title page of the play in NLI 30,006: Mark writes, "This begins new / Volume IV."

In some respects, the *Helmet* plays seem to be anomalies among the other plays Yeats wrote between 1900 and 1910. Farce, and comedy more generally, were not modes that Yeats used frequently, and the non-naturalistic style of the plays, with their striking Red Man and vivid color scheme, seem to look forward to his experiments with movement and more stylized staging in his theatre of the teens and twenties.

Yet the present edition reveals the way that these plays—and especially the revision from *The Golden Helmet* to *The Green Helmet*—help to bridge two phases in Yeats's career. In 1907, as he was writing *The Golden Helmet,* Yeats was beginning to envision a move away from the Abbey and back to the writing of lyric verse. By the time *The Green Helmet* was completed, around New Year's Day 1910, he was envisioning the play as the centerpiece of his first new volume of lyrics since *In the Seven Woods* (1903). The *Helmet* plays connect the commercial theater manager of 1904–1907 to the burgeoning modernist experimenter of 1910–1916.

The present volume builds on the invaluable work of S. B. Bushrui in *Yeats's Verse Plays: The Revisions, 1900–1910* (Oxford: Clarendon Press, 1965). Any reader interested in the *Helmet* plays should also consult that book, which charts the revision of several key passages

[42]W. B. Yeats, *The Green Helmet and Other Poems* (Dundrum: Cuala Press, 1910), p. 28.

[43]See Part II, p. 109, below.

from prose into verse, commenting especially on how the revision shifts the play's thematic emphases. But since Bushrui's work was published, more material has become easily available to scholars, especially the Oxford University Press's edition of Yeats's letters, which allow for a more precise dating of the processes of revision than was previously possible. Moreover, in photographically reproducing a complete manuscript draft of *The Green Helmet*, the present volume allows readers to see not only the thematic development of the plays but also Yeats's characteristic process of writing and rewriting, his struggles with versification in some passages, and the step-by-step evolution of characters and scenes.

The two plays considered in the present edition, and particularly the process of rewriting that accounts for the differences between them, help to reveal some of the impulses in Yeats's imagination at a crucial moment of transition in his career. What began as his "bubble blown in three days" became an experiment in verse drama that charts new ideas about Irish politics, about his relationship with Maud Gonne, about the aesthetics of the drama. The transition from *The Golden Helmet* to *The Green Helmet*—which this edition illuminates—mirrors Yeats's own transitions from his Abbey years into the great decades of his mature poetic career.

Transcription Principles and Procedures

This edition traces the evolution of *The Golden Helmet* and *The Green Helmet* through three distinct phases of development: the composition and publication of *The Golden Helmet* in 1907–1908; the composition of *The Green Helmet* between 1908 and 1910; and the revision of *The Green Helmet* for the publication of *Collected Plays* in 1934. Complete holograph manuscripts survive for only one of these three phases (NLI 8761, probably dating from January 1910), but this volume attempts to reproduce all extant manuscript material, including corrected proofs where holograph manuscripts do not survive. For holograph manuscripts, the edition provides photographic reproductions of each manuscript page, with a transcription facing. In the case of proof sheets, only pages that have been significantly marked with corrections have been reproduced photographically; clean or very lightly marked pages have generally been transcribed or represented in an apparatus criticus collating variant readings.

In general, where Yeats has written on a page, whether that page is part of a holograph manuscript or part of a proof, the reader of this volume can see a photograph of the source page for the facing transcription. Nevertheless, Yeats's hand is notoriously difficult to decipher in places, and so to retain consistency, this edition has adopted several conventions in transcribing his writing:

1. Yeats commonly broke words off or did not complete words in his manuscripts, especially when he was working quickly. In the transcriptions, incomplete words are reproduced as written, in their incomplete state.

2. For the long fourteeners of *The Green Helmet*, line breaks and indentation have been preserved as closely as possible, both in the autograph manuscript NLI 8761 and in the proof sheets of that play.

3. Errors and inconsistencies in spelling and capitalization have been preserved *literatim*.

4. Ink holograph script is transcribed in normal roman font. Any markings in pencil are in *italics*. Several of the proof sheets reproduced in this edition contain autograph corrections by both Yeats and Thomas Mark at Macmillan. Where that is the case, the printed text is transcribed in **roman boldface**; Yeats's markings are in normal roman font; and Mark's markings are represented in an unmistakably different font.

5. Symbols for illegible words and editorial conjectures:

[?]	a totally illegible word
[? ? ?]	several totally illegible words, with the number of question marks corresponding to the apparent number of words
[~~?~~]	a canceled and totally illegible word
[?the]	a conjectural reading
[?the/?then]	equally possible conjectural readings

6. Cancellation of single lines or of words within a line is indicated by horizontal cancellation lines. (These lines are straight even where Yeats's lines were wavy.) Occasionally, Yeats canceled a word or phrase and then later canceled the line or part of several lines. In such cases the word or phrase struck through initially is canceled in the transcription with a diagonal or wavy line and the line or part of several lines with horizontal lines, as illustrated.

canceled ~~in the transcription with a diagonal or wavy line~~

Where Yeats intended to cancel an entire word but struck through only part of it, the cancellation line in the transcription extends through the entire word. However, even when it seems likely that Yeats meant to cancel an entire phrase or line, no word that he did not at least partially cancel is canceled in the transcriptions.

7. Cancellation of entire passages is indicated by vertical brackets in the left margin.

8. The following abbreviations have been used in *apparatus criticus* entries:

sd	stage direction
del	deleted
rev to	revised to

9. Omitted from the *apparatus criticus* are variants involving the exchange of "and" for "&" and variants of type style, spacing, underlining, and punctuation in titles and in speaker identifications, unless not to do so would create an ambiguity.

10. In Yeats's handwriting, it is often difficult to distinguish lowercase letters from uppercase ones, especially in the case of "a," "o," "w," and "s." An initial capital "a," for example, can be written as a block capital "A" or as a slightly larger scripted lower-case letter. In these transcriptions, where these letters begin lines of verse, thay have been transcribed as uppercase, in accordance with Yeats's habit of capitalizing the first word in each line of verse and part ascription.

11. Yeats's drafts occasionally include blots that may have been made accidentally. In cases where their significance has not been determined, they are silently omitted.

Part I

The Golden Helmet. 1908

Galley Proof of the Quinn Edition. NYPL

Yeats asked his friend John Quinn, the American attorney and art patron, to publish a small edition of *The Golden Helmet* in New York in order to secure the American copyright. Quinn's edition of fifty copies (Wade 74) appeared in June 1908, four months before the play's first English appearance in volume 4 of the Shakespeare Head Press's *Collected Works in Verse and Prose* (Wade 78). Autograph manuscripts of *The Golden Helmet* do not survive, so the galley proofs transcribed here, which Yeats read, represent the earliest manuscript witness for the play. Except for two variants, indicated in notes to the transcription, the text of the galleys is identical to the one published in *The Golden Helmet* (New York, 1908; Wade 74).

NYPL, Galleys 1–6

[1]

THE GOLDEN HELMET

PERSONS IN THE PLAY

CUCHULAIN
LEAGERIE
EMER, *Cuchulain's wife*
LEAGERIE'S WIFE
CONAL'S WIFE
LAEG, *Cuchulain's chariot-driver*
RED MAN
HORSEBOYS AND SCULLIONS
THREE BLACK MEN

A house made of logs. There are two windows at the back and a door which cuts off one of the corners of the room. Through the door one can see rocks, which make the ground outside the door higher than it is within, and the sea. Through the windows one can see nothing but the sea. There are three great chairs at the opposite side to the door, with a table before them. There are cups and a flagon of ale on the table.

At the Abbey Theatre the house is orange red, and the chairs, tables, and flagons black, with a slight purple tinge which is not clearly distinguishable from the black. The rocks are black, with a few green touches. The sea is green and luminous, and all the characters, except the* RED MAN *and the Black Men, are dressed in various tints of green, one or two with touches of purple which looks nearly black. The* Black Men *are in dark purple and the* RED MAN *is altogether dressed in red. He is very tall and his height is increased by horns on the Golden Helmet. The Helmet has in reality more dark green than gold about it. The* Black Men *have cats' heads painted on their black cloth caps. The effect is intentionally violent and startling.

---

found in NYPL
published *The Golden Helmet* (New York: John Quinn, 1908)
The Collected Works in Verse and Prose (Stratford: Shakespeare Head Press, 1908)

CONAL.

Not a sail, not a wave, and if the sea were not purring a little like a cat, not a sound. There is no danger yet. I can see a long way for the moonlight is on the sea. [*A horn sounds*.

LEAGERIE.

Ah, there is something.

CONAL.

It must be from the land, and it is from the sea that danger comes. We need not be afraid of anything that comes from the land. [*Looking out of door*.] I cannot see anybody, the rocks and the trees hide a great part of the pathway upon that side.

LEAGERIE. [*sitting at table*].

It sounded like Cuchulain's horn, but that's not possible.

CONAL.

Yes, that's impossible. He will never come home from Scotland. He has all he wants there. Luck in all he does. Victory and wealth and happiness flowing in on him, while here at home all goes to rack, and a man's good name drifts away between night and morning.

LEAGERIE.

I wish he would come home for all that, and put quiet and respect for those that are more than she is into that young wife of his. Only this very night your wife and my wife had to forbid her to go into the dining-hall before them. She is young, and she is Cuchulain's wife, and so she must spread her tail like a peacock.

CONAL [*at door*].

I can see the horn blower now, a young man wrapped in a cloak.

LEAGERIE.

Do not let him come in. Tell him to go elsewhere for shelter. This is no place to seek shelter in.

CONAL.

That is right. I will tell him to go away, for nobody must know the disgrace that is to fall upon Ireland this night.

LEAGERIE.

Nobody of living men but us two must ever

[1, continued]

know that.

CONAL [*outside door*].

Go away, go away!

[A YOUNG MAN *covered by a long cloak is standing upon the rocks outside the door.*

YOUNG MAN.

I am a traveler, and I am looking for sleep and food.

CONAL.

A law has been made that nobody is to come into this house to-night.

YOUNG MAN.

Who made that law?

CONAL.

We two made it, and who has so good a right? for we have to guard this house and to keep it from robbery, and from burning, and from enchantment.

YOUNG MAN.

Then I will unmake the law. Out of my way!

[He struggles with* CONAL *and shoves past into the house.

[2]

CONAL.

I thought no living man but Leagerie could have stood against me; and Leagerie himself could not have shoved past me. What is more, no living man could if I were not taken by surprise. How could I expect to find so great a strength?

LEAGERIE.

Go out of this: there is another house a little further along the shore; our wives are there with their servants, and they will give you food and drink.

YOUNG MAN.

It is in this house I will have food and drink.

LEAGERIE [*drawing his sword*].

Go out of this, or I will make you.

[*The* YOUNG MAN *seizes* LEAGAIRE'S *arm, and thrusting it up, passes him, and puts his shield*

over the chair, where there is an empty place.

YOUNG MAN [*at table*].

It is here I will spend the night, but I won't tell you why until I have drunk. I am thirsty. What, the flagon full and the cups empty and Leagerie and Conal there! Why, what's in the wind that Leagerie and Conal cannot drink?

LEAGERIE.

It is Cuchulain.

CONAL.

Better go away to Scotland, again, of if you stay here ask no one what has happened or what is going to happen.

CUCHULAIN.

What more is there that can happen so strange as that I should come home after years and that you should bid me begone?

CONAL.

I tell you that this is no fit house to welcome you, for it is a disgraced house.

CUCHULAIN.

What is it you are hinting at? You were sitting there with ale beside you and the door open, and quarrelsome thoughts. You are waiting for something or someone. It is for some messenger who is to bring you some spoil, or to some adventure that you will keep for yourselves.

LEAGERIE.

Better tell him, for he has such luck that it may be his luck will amend ours.

CONAL.

Yes, I had better tell him, for even now at this very door we saw what luck he had. He had the slope of the ground to help him. Is the sea quiet?

LEAGERIE [*looks out of window*].

There is nothing stirring.

CONAL.

Cuchulain, a little after you went out of this country we were sitting here drinking. We were merry. It was late, close on to midnight, when a strange-looking man with red hair and a great sword in his hand came in through that door. He asked for ale and we gave it to him, for we were tired of drinking with one another.

[2, continued]

He became very merry, and for every joke we made he made a better, and presently we all three got up and danced, and then we sang, and then he said he would show us a new game. He said he would stoop down and that one of us was to cut off his head, and afterwards one of us, or whoever has a mind for the game, was to stoop down and have his head whipped off. 'You take off my head,' said he, 'and then I take off his head, and that will be a bargain and a debt between us. A head for a head, that is the game,' said he. We laughed at him and told him he was drunk, for how could he whip off a head when his own had been whipped off? Then he began abusing us and calling us names, so I ran at him and cut his head off, and the head went on laughing where it lay, and presently he caught it up in his hands and ran out and plunged into the sea.

CUCHULAIN [*laughs*].

I have imagined as good, when I had as much ale, and believed it too.

LEAGERIE [*at table*].

I tell you, Cuchulain, you never did. You never imagined a story like this.

CONAL.

Why must you be always putting yourself up against Leagerie and myself? and what is more, it was no imagination at all. We said to ourselves that all came out of the flagon, and we laughed, and we said we will tell nobody about it. We made an oath to tell nobody. But twelve months after when we were sitting by this table, the flagon between us—

LEAGERIE.

But full up to the brim

CONAL.

The thought of that story had put us from our drinking.

LEAGERIE.

We were telling it over to one another.

---

122 The word "very" was omitted in Quinn's published edition of *The Golden Helmet*.

[3]

CONAL.

Suddenly that man came in with his head on his shoulders again, and the big sword in his hand. He asked for payment of his debt, and because neither I nor Leagerie would let him cut off our heads he began abusing us and making little of us, and saying that we were a disgrace, and that all Ireland was disgraced because of us. We had not a word to say.

LEAGERIE.

If you had been here you would have been as silent as we were.

CONAL.

At last he said he would come in again in twelve months and give us one more chance to keep our word and pay our debt. After that he went down into the sea again. Will he tell the whole world of the disgrace that has come upon us, do you think?

CUCHULAIN.

Whether he does or does not, we will stand there in the door with our swords out and drive him down to the sea again.

CONAL.

What is the use of fighting with a man whose head laughs when it has been cut off?

LEAGERIE.

We might run away, but he would follow us everywhere.

CONAL.

He is coming; the sea is beginning to splash and rumble as it did before he came the last time.

CUCHULAIN.

Let us shut the door and put our backs against it.

LEAGERIE.

It is too late. Look, there he is at the door. He is standing on the threshold.

[A man dressed in red, with a great sword and red, ragged hair, and having a Golden Helmet on his head, is standing on the threshold.

CUCHULAIN.

Go back into the sea, old red head! If you will take off heads, take off the head of the sea

[3, continued]

turtle of Muirthemne, or of the pig of Connaught that has a moon in his belly, or of that old juggler Mannnan, son of the sea, or of the red man of the Boyne, or of the King of the Cats, for they are of your own sort, and it may be they understand your ways. Go, I say, for when a man's head is off it does not grow again. What are you standing there for? Go down, I say. If I cannot harm you with the sword I will put you down into the sea with my hands. Do you laugh at me, old red head? Go down before I lay my hands upon you.

RED MAN.

So you also believe I was in earnest when I asked for a man's head? It was but a drinker's joke, an old juggling feat, to pass the time. I am the best of all drinkers and tipsy companions, the kindest there is among the Shape-changers of the world. Look, I have brought the Golden Helmet as a gift. It is for you or for Leagerie or for Conal, for the best man, and the bravest fighting-man amongst you, and you yourselves shall choose the man. Leagerie is brave, and Conal is brave. They risk their lives in battle, but they were not brave enough for my jokes and my juggling. [*He lays the Golden Helmet on the ground.]* Have I been too grim a joker? Well, I am forgiven now, for there is the Helmet, and let the strongest take it.

[*He goes out.*

CONAL [*taking Helmet*].

It is my right. I am a year older than Leagerie, and I have fought in more battles.

LEAGERIE [*strutting about stage, sings*].

Leagerie of the Battles
Has put to the sword
The cat-headed men
And carried away
Their hidden gold.

[*He snatches Helmet at the last word.*

CONAL.

Give it back to me, I say. What was the treasure but withered leaves when you got to

your own door?

CUCHULAIN.

[*Taking the Helmet from* LEAGERIE.] Give it to me, I say.

[4]

CONAL.

You are too young, Cuchulain. What deeds have you to be set beside our deeds?

CUCHULAIN.

I have not taken it for myself. It will belong to us all equally. [He goes to table and begins filling Helmet with ale.] We will pass it round and drink out of it turn about and no one will be able to claim that it belongs to him more than another. I drink to your wife, Conal, and to your wife, Leagerie, and I drink to Emer my own wife. [*Shouting and blowing of horns in the distance.]* What is that noise?

CONAL.

It is the horseboys and the huntboys and the scullions quarrelling. I know the sound, for I have heard it often of late. It is a good thing that you are home, Cuchulain, for it is your own horseboy and chariot-driver Laeg, that is the worst of all, and now you will keep him quiet. They take down the great hunting-horns when they cannot drown one another's voices by shouting. There—there—do you hear them now? [*Shouting so as to be heard above the noise*.] I drink to your good health, Cuchulain, and to your young wife, though it were well if she did not quarrel with my wife.

Many men, among whom is LAEG chariot-driver of CUCHULAIN, come in with great horns of many fantastic shapes.

LAEG.

I am Cuchulain's chariot-drive, and I say that my master is the best.

ANOTHER.

He is not, but Leagerie is.

ANOTHER.

No, but Conal is.

LAEG.

Make them listen to me, Cuchulain.

[4, continued]

ANOTHER

No, but listen to me.

LAEG.

When I said Cuchulain should have the Helmet, they blew the horns.

ANOTHER.

Conal has it. The best man has it.

CUCHULAIN.

Silence, all of you. What is all this uproar, Laeg, and who began it?

[The Scullions and the Horseboys point at LAEG and cry, 'He began it.' They keep up an all but continual murmur through what follows.

LAEG.

A man with a red beard came where we were sitting, and as he passed me he cried out that they were taking a golden helmet or some such thing from you and denying you the championship of Ireland. I stood up on that and I cried out that you were the best of the men of Ireland. But the others cried out for Leagerie or Conal, and because I have a big voice, and as neither I nor they would keep silent we have to come here to settle it. I demand that the Helmet be taken from Conal and given to you.

[The* Horeseboys *and the* Scullions *shout, 'No, no; give it to Leagerie,' 'The best man has it,' etc.

CUCHULAIN.

It has not been given to Conal or to anyone. I have made it into a drinking-cup that it may belong to all. I drank and then Conal drank. Give it to Leagerie, Conal, that he may drink. That will make them see that it belongs to all of us.

A SCULLION OR HORSEBOY.

Cuchulain is right.

ANOTHER.

Cucuhlain is right, and I am tired of blowing on the big horn.

LAEG.

Cuchulain, you drank first.

ANOTHER.

He gives it to Leagerie now, but he has taken the honour for himself. Did you hear him say he drank first? He claimed to be the best by drinking first.

ANOTHER.

Did Cuchulain drink the first?

LAEG [*triumphantly*].

You drank the first, Cuchulain.

CONAL.

Did you claim to be better than us by drinking first?

[5]

[LEAGERIE *and* CONAL *draw their swords*.

CUCHULAIN.

Is it that old dried herring, that old red juggler who has made us quarrel for his own comfort? [*The* Horseboys *and the* Scullions *murmur excitedly*.] He gave the Helmet to set us by the hears, and because we would not quarrel over it, he goes to Laeg and tells him that I am wronged. Who knows where he is now, or who he is stirring up to make mischief between us? Go back to your work and do not stir from it whatever noise comes to you or whatever shape shows itself.

A SCULLION.

Cuchulain is right. I am tired blowing on the big horn.

CUCHULAIN.

Go in silence.

[*The Scullions and the Horseboys turn towards the door, but stand still on hearing the voice of* LEAGERIE'S WIFE *outside the door*.

LEAGERIE'S WIFE.

My man is the best. I will go in the first. I will go in the first.

EMER.

My man is the best, and I will go in first.

CONAL'S WIFE.

No, for my man is the best, and it is I that should go first.

[LEAGERIE'S WIFE *and* CONAL'S WIFE *struggle in the doorway*.

[5, continued]

LEAGERIE'S WIFE ***sings.***

My man is the best
What other has fought
The cat-headed man
That mew in the sea
And carried away
Their long-hidden gold?
They struck with their claws
And bit with their teeth,
But Leagerie my husband
Put all to the sword.

CONAL'S WIFE.

[Putting her hand over the other's mouth and getting in front of her.]

My husband has fought
With strong men in armour
Had he a quarrel
With cats, it is certain
He'd war with none
But the stout and heavy
With good claws on them.
What glory in warring
With hollow shadows
That helplessly mew?

EMER.

[Thrusting herself between them and forcing both of them back with her hands.]

I am Emer, wife of Cuchulain, and no one shall go in front of me, or sing in front of me, or praise any that I have not a mind to hear praised.

[CUCHULAIN ***puts his spear across the door.***

CUCHULAIN.

All of our three wives shall come in together, and by three doors equal in height and in breadth and in honour. Break down the bottoms of the windows.

[While* CONAL *and* LEAGERIE *are breaking down the bottoms of the windows each of their wives goes to the window where her husband is. While the windows are being broken down

EMER ***sings.***

My man is the best
And Conal's wife

And the wife of Leagerie
Know that they lie
When they praise their own
Out of envy of me.
My man is the best,
First for his own sake,
Being the bravest
And handsomest man
And the most beloved
By the women of Ireland
That envy me,
And then for his wife's sake
Because I'm the youngest
And handsomest queen.

[*When the windows have been made into doors,* CUCHULAIN *takes his spear from the door where* EMER *is, and all three come in at the same moment.*

EMER.

I am come to praise you and to put courage into you, Cuchulain, as a wife should, that they may not take the championship of the men of Ireland from you.

LEAGERIE'S WIFE.

You lie, Emer, for it is Cuchulain and Conal who are taking the championship from my husband.

CONAL'S WIFE.

Cuchulain has taken it.

[6]

CUCHULAIN.

Townland against townland, barony against barony, kingdom against kingdom, province against province, and if there be but two door-posts to a door the one fighting against the other. [*He takes up the Helmet which* LEAGERIE *had laid down upon the table when he went to break out the bottom of the window.*] This Helmet will bring no more wars into Ireland. [*He throws it into the sea.*]

LEAGERIE'S WIFE.

You have done that to rob my husband.

CONAL'S WIFE

You could not keep it for yourself, and so

[6, continued]

you threw it away that nobody else might have it.

CONAL.

You should not have done that, Cuchulain.

LEAGERIE.

You have done us a great wrong.

EMER.

Who is for Cuchulain?

CUCHULAIN.

Let no one stir.

EMER.

Who is for Cuchulain, I say?

[*She draws her dagger from her belt and sings the same words as before, flourishing it about. While she has been singing,* **CONAL'S WIFE** *and* **LEAGERIE'S WIFE** *have drawn their daggers and run at her to kill her, but* **CUCHULAIN** *has forced them back.* **CONAL** *and* **LEAGERIE** *have drawn their swords to strike* **CUCHULAIN.**

CONAL'S WIFE.

[*While* **EMER** *is still singing.*]

Silence her voice, silence her voice, blow the horns, make a noise!

[*The* **Scullions** *and* **Horseboys** *blow their horns or fight among themselves. There is a deafen- ing noise and a confused fight. Suddenly three black hands upon black arms holding extinguishers come through the window and extinguish the torches. It is now pitch dark but for a very faint light outside the house which merely shows that there are moving forms, but not who or what they are, and in the darkness one can hear low terrified voices.*

FIRST VOICE.

Did you see them putting out the torches?

ANOTHER VOICE.

They came up out of the sea, three black men.

ANOTHER VOICE.

They have heads of cats upon them.

ANOTHER VOICE.

They came up mewing out of the sea.

ANOTHER VOICE.

How dark it is! one of them has put his

hand over the moon.

~~ANOTHER.~~

~~They must have put out the stars.~~

[*A light gradually comes into the windows as if shining from the sea. The* **RED MAN** *is seen standing in the midst of the house.*

RED MAN.

I demand the debt that is owing. I demand that some man shall stoop down that I may cut his head off as my head was cut off. If my debt is not paid, no peace shall come to Ireland, and Ireland shall lie weak before her enemies. But if my debt is paid there shall be peace.

CUCHULAIN.

The quarrels of Ireland shall end. What is one man's life? I will pay the debt with my own head. [EMER ***wails.*****] Do not cry out, Emer, for it I were not myself, if I were not Cuchulain, one of those that God has made reckless, the women of Ireland had not loved me, and you had not held your head so high. [*****He stoops, bending his head. Three Black Men come to the door. Two hold torches, and one stooping between them holds up the Golden Helmet. The*** **RED MAN** ***gives one of the Black Men his sword and takes the Helmet.*****] What do you wait for, old man? Come, raise up your sword!**

RED MAN.

I will not harm you, Cuchulain. I am the guardian of this land, and age after age I come up out of the sea to try the men of Ireland. I give you the championship because you are without fear, and you shall win many battles with laughing lips and endure wounding and betrayal without bitterness of heart; and when men gaze upon you, their hearts shall grow greater and their minds clear; until the day come~~s~~ when I darken your minds that there may be an end to the story, and a song on the harp-string.

END.

---

392 Part name and line were omitted in Quinn's edition of *The Golden Helmet* (New York, 1908).

Part II

The Green Helmet (An Heroic Farce). Late 1909–1934

The Helmet—An Heroic Farce. Holograph Draft (late 1909). NLI 8761

Soon after the first performance of *The Golden Helmet,* on March 19, 1908, Yeats began revising the play into verse, working in the fourteeners he had admired in Wilfrid Scawen Blunt's play *Fand of the Fair Cheek*, which had been performed at the Abbey. By late December 1909 Yeats wrote to Lady Gregory that he would complete the revision with three days' work (WBY to LG, December 22, 1909, *CL* Archive, accession number 1249). The manuscript reproduced and transcribed here probably dates from that period; note that the title is given as *The Helmet* and has not yet been changed to *The Green Helmet*.

Characteristically, Yeats composed *The Green Helmet* on the recto pages of an exercise book, using the verso pages to work out problematic passages or to resolve metrical difficulties. The manuscript transcribed here represents, for Yeats, a very clean copy. The most interesting exceptions are at the end of the play, as we can see Yeats struggling with Emer's song on folios 25^v, 26^r, and 26^v. We know from Yeats's correspondence that Emer's song was among the last portions of the play to be worked out to his satisfaction, so it is probable that this manuscript is a late autograph draft. Earlier autograph drafts do not survive.

The variants between NLI 8761 and *The Green Helmet*'s first book printing in *The Green Helmet and Other Poems* (Dundrum: Cuala Press, 1910) are collated below the transcriptions.

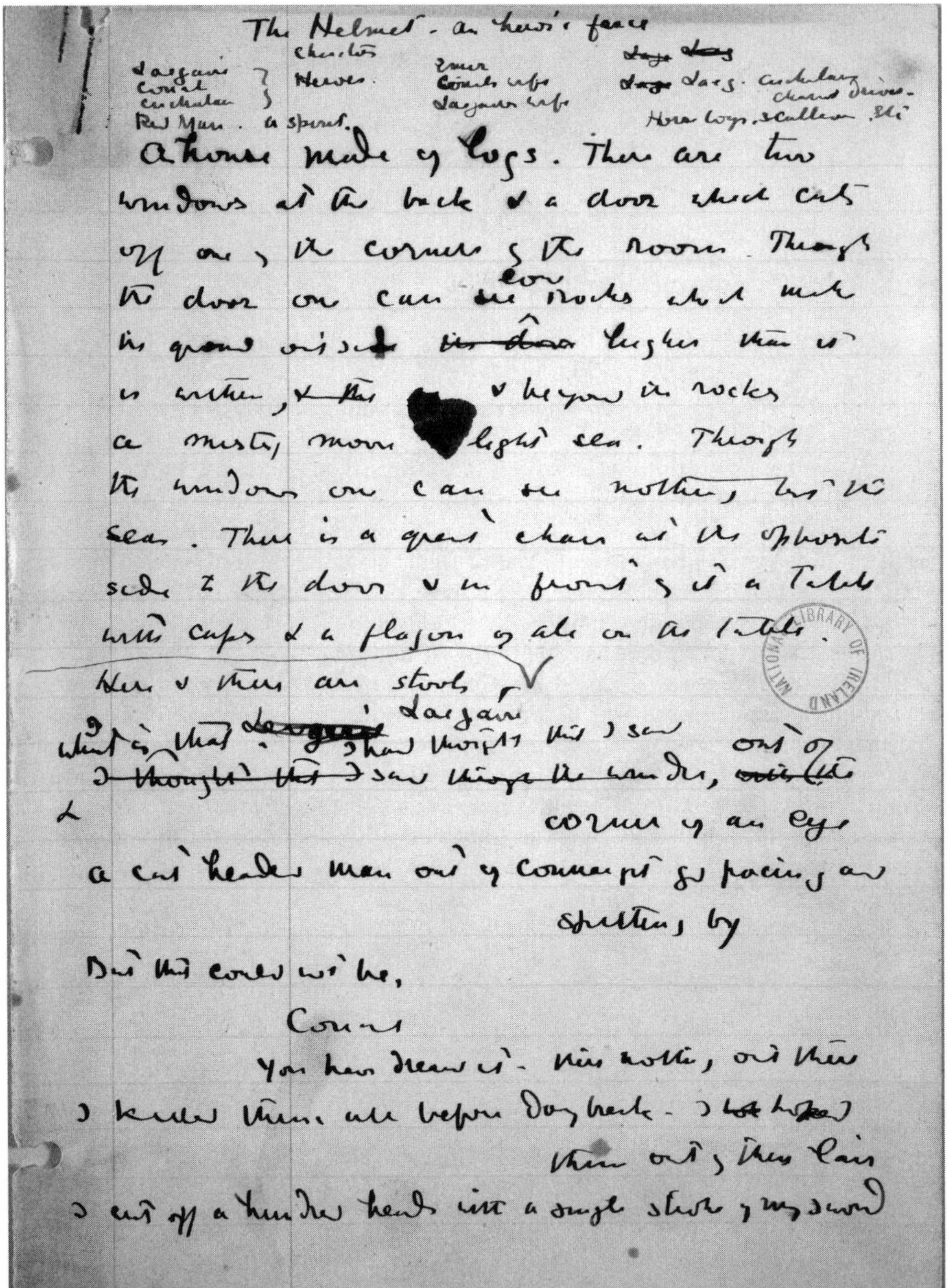
The Helmet - an heroic farce

Charioteers

Laegaire, Conall, Cuchulain } Heroes. Emer, Conall's wife, Laegaire's wife. Laegaire's. Cuchulain's chariot driver. Red Man. a spirit. Horse boys, scullions, etc

A house made of logs. There are two windows at the back & a door which cuts off one of the corners of the room. Through the door one can see rocks which make the ground outside higher than it is within, & beyond the rocks a misty moonlight sea. Through the windows one can see nothing but the sea. There is a great chair at the opposite side to the door & in front of it a table with cups & a flagon of ale on the table. Here & there are stools.

Laegaire

What is that? I had thought that I saw out of the corner of an eye a cat headed man out of Connaught go pacing and spitting by. But that could not be.

Conall

You have dreamt it - there's nothing out there I killed them all before day break - I hunted them out of their lairs I cut off a hundred heads with a single stroke of my sword

[NLI 8761, 1[r]]

The Helmet – an heroic farce
Characters

Laegaire Conal Cuchulan	} Heroes	Emer Conals wife Laegaires wife	~~Lage~~ ~~Laeg~~ ~~Lage~~ Laeg. Cuchulain's chariot driver Horse boys, scullions, Etc
Red Man.	A spirit		

A house made of logs. There are two windows at the back & a door which cuts off one of the corners of the room. Through the door one can see ^low^ rocks which make the ground outside ~~the door~~ higher than it is within, ~~& the~~ & beyond the rocks a misty moon light sea. Through the windows one can see nothing but the sea. There is a great chair at the opposite side to the door & in front of it is a table with cups & a flagon of ale on the table. Here & there are stools.

---

title The Helmet – an heroic farce] THE GREEN HELMET / An Heroic Farce *Cuala*

dramatis personae Characters] THE PERSONS OF THE PLAY *Cuala* Heroes *and brace lacking in Cuala* Conal] CONALL *Cuala* Cuchulan] CUCHULAIN *Cuala* Conals wife] CONALL'S WIFE *Cuala* LAEGAIRE'S WIFE *Cuala* Laeg.] Laeg, *Cuala* Horse boys, scullions, etc.] HORSE BOYS AND SCULLIONS / BLACK MEN, etc. *Cuala*

scene A house] SCENE: A house *Cuala* & a door] and a door *Cuala* moon light] moon-lit *Cuala* & a door] and a door *Cuala* door one] door, one *Cuala* & beyond] and beyond *Cuala* moon light] moon-lit *Cuala* door & in front of it is a table with cups & a flagon of ale on the table] door, and in front of it a table with cups and a flagon of ale *Cuala* *new paragraph after* stools. *as follows*

At the Abbey Theatre the house is orange red and the chairs and tables and flagons black, with a slight purple tinge which is not clearly distinguishable from the black. The rocks are black with a few green touches. The sea is green and luminous and all the characters except the Red Man and the Black Men are dressed in various shades of green, one or two with touches of purple which look nearly black. The Black Men all wear dark purple and have eared caps, and at the end their eyes should look green from the reflected light of the sea. The Red Man is altogether in red. He is very tall, and his height increased by horns on the Green Helmet. The effect is intentionally violent and startling. *Cuala*

In the first published version of *The Green Helmet* (Dundrum: Cuala Press, 1910; Wade 84), and in every subsequent edition, the stage direction includes a second section (omitted in this manuscript) about the first production of the play at the Abbey. (See the entry following "there are stools." in the *apparatus criticus* above). The insertion point visible at the end of the stage direction in the facing photograph may have pointed to an attachment to this sheet, now missing, that contained the rest of the stage direction. This conjecture is supported by the rust stain from a paper-clip visible in the top left of the manuscript page, which suggests that an attachment had at one time been clipped to this sheet.

dramatis personae WBY's spelling of character names is erratic, both from haste and uncertainty, throughout this manuscript. The transcription presents what WBY wrote; the printed variants in dialogue and stage directions are recorded in the *apparatus criticus*; but we have not recorded the numerous corrections to part ascriptions in *Cuala*, which unfailingly reproduces the spellings shown for *Cuala* under "dramatis personae" in the notes above.

[NLI 8761, 1r]

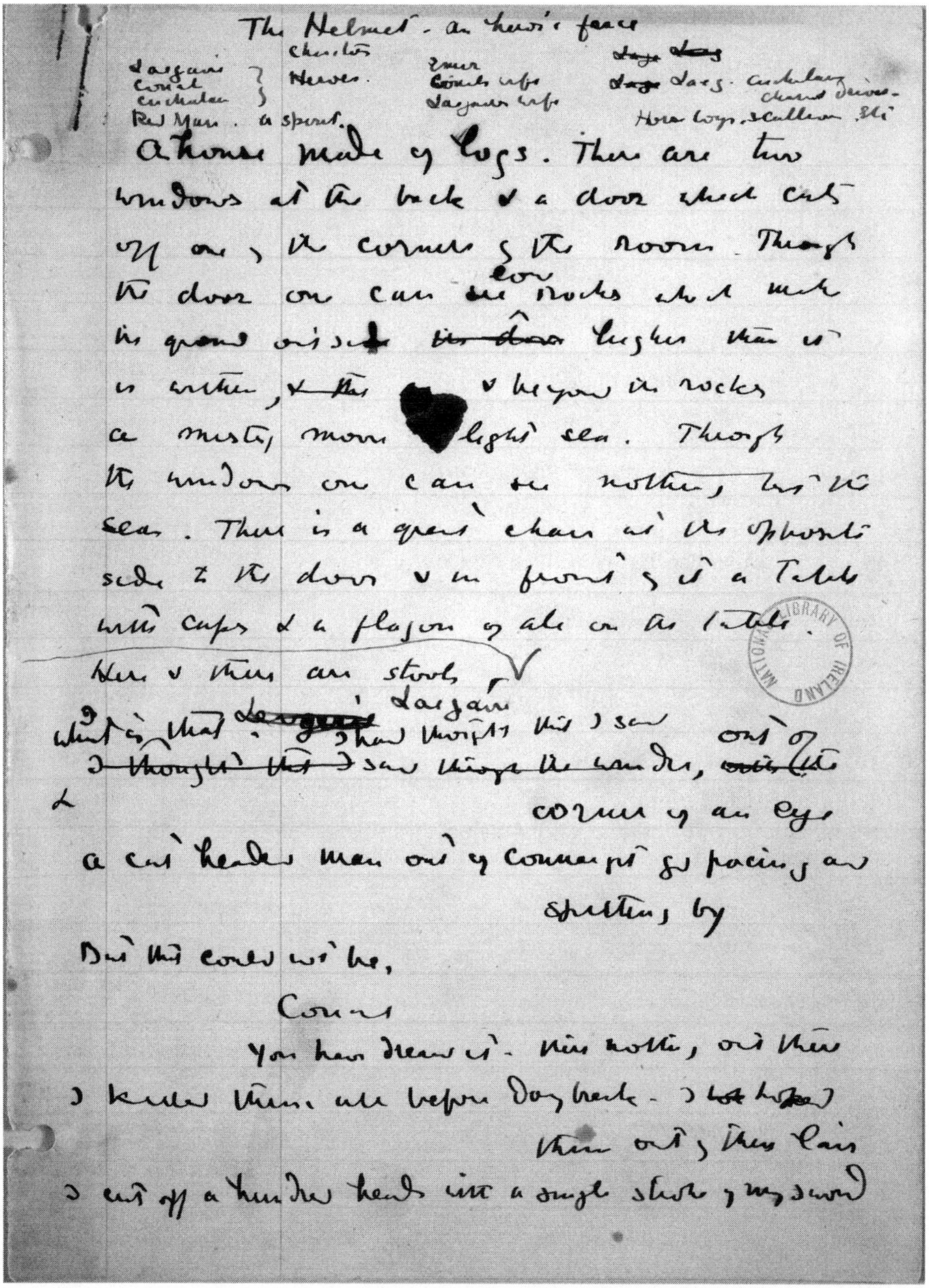

The Helmet – an heroic farce

Characters

Laegaire / Conal / Cuchulain } Heroes.
Red Man. a spirit.
Emer / Conal's wife / Laegaire's wife
~~Laeg~~ ~~Laeg~~ ~~Laeg~~ Laeg. Cuchulain's chariot driver.
Horse boys, scullions, etc

A house made of logs. There are two windows at the back & a door which cuts off one of the corners of the room. Through the door one can see ~~see~~ low rocks which make the ground outside ~~the door~~ higher than it is within, & ~~the~~ & beyond the rocks a misty moon light sea. Through the windows one can see nothing but the sea. There is a great chair at the opposite side to the door & in front of it a Table with cups & a flagon of ale on the table.

Here & there are stools,

What is that. ~~Laegaire~~ Laegaire I have thought that I saw ~~I thought that~~ I saw through the window, out of the corner of an eye a cut headed man out of Connacht go pacing and spitting by

But that could not be,

Conal

You have dreamt it – there is nothing out there I killed them all before daybreak – I ~~hunted~~ hunted them out of their lairs I cut off a hundred heads with a single stroke of my sword

[NLI 8761, 1[r], continued]

Laegaire
~~Laegaire~~
What is that I had thought that I saw out of
1 ^ ~~I thought that I~~ saw ~~through the window~~, ~~with the~~ [1–5]
corner of an eye
2 A cat headed man out of Connaight go pacing and
spitting by
3 But this could not be.

Conal
4 You have dreamed it. There's nothing out there
5 I killed them all before daybreak. I ~~hok~~ hoked
them out of their lair
6 I cut off a hundred heads with a single stroke of my sword

---

1 I had thought that I saw out of the corner of an eye] I had thought that I saw, though but in the wink of an eye? *Cuala*
2 cat headed] cat-headed *Cuala* Connaight] Connaught *Cuala* spitting by] spitting by; *Cuala*
3 this] that *Cuala*
4 Conal] Conall *Cuala* dreamed it. There's] dreamed it—there's *Cuala*
5 daybreak. I hoked] daybreak—I hoked *Cuala* lair] lair; *Cuala*
6 sword] sword, *Cuala*

Numbers in brackets at the right of each manuscript page are the corresponding line numbers in *VPl*, pp. 422–453.

4 The change in spelling from "Conal" to "Conall" is uniform throughout *Cuala* and will not be noted hereafter in the *apparatus criticus*.

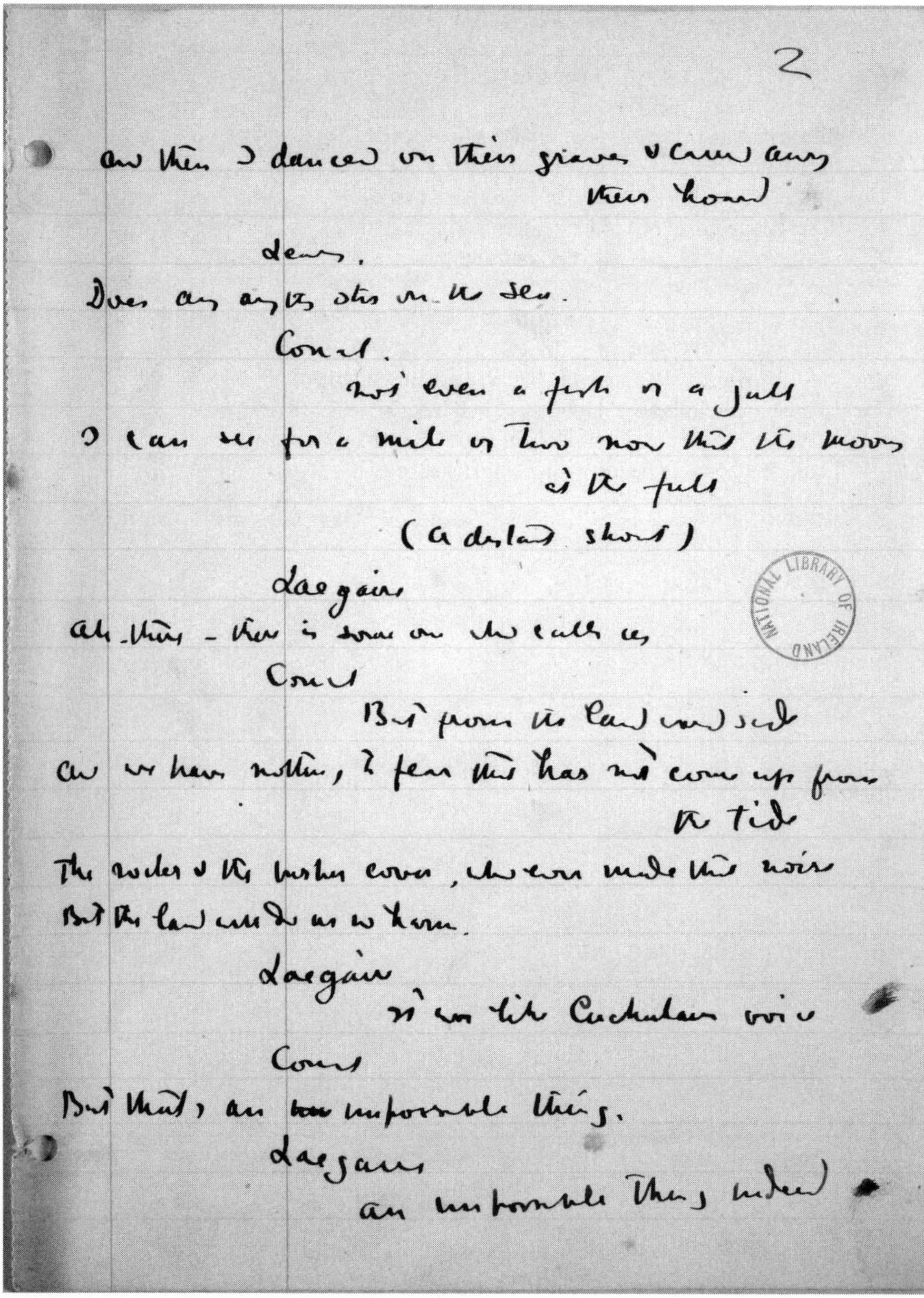
2

and then I danced on their graves & carried away
their hoard

Leary.
Does any anything stir on the sea.

Conall.
Not even a fish or a gull
I can see for a mile or two now that the moon
is at the full

(A distant shout)

Laegaire
Ah there — there is some one who calls us

Conall
But from the land or sea
And we have nothing, I fear that has not come up from
the tide
The rocks & the bushes cover, whoever made that noise
But the land will do us no harm.

Laegaire
It was like Cuchulain's voice

Conall
But that's an impossible thing.

Laegaire
An impossible thing indeed

[NLI 8761, 2^{r}]

2

1 And then I danced on their graves & carried away
their hoard [6–13]

Laegaire

2 Does anything stir on the sea.

Conal

3 Not even a fish or a gull
4 I can see for a mile or two now that the moons
at the full

(a distant shout)

Laegaire

5 Ah – there – there is some one who calls us

Conal

6 But from the landward side
7 And we have nothing to fear that has not come up from
the tide
8 The rocks & the bushes cover, whoever made that noise
9 But the land will do us no harm.

Laegaire

10 It was like Cuchulain's voice

Conal

11 But that's an ~~un~~ impossible thing.

Laegaire

12 An impossible thing indeed

---

1 graves & carried] graves and carried] *Cuala* hoard] hoard. *Cuala*
2 sea.] sea? *Cuala*
4 two now] two, now *Cuala* full] full. *Cuala*
5 calls us] calls us. *Cuala*
6 side] side, *Cuala*
7 tide] tide; *Cuala*
8 rocks & the bushes cover,] rocks and the bushes cover *Cuala* noise] noise, *Cuala*
9 harm.] harm, *Cuala*
10 voice] voice. *Cuala*
12 indeed] indeed. *Cuala*

10, 12 The ink smudges in the right margin appear to be accidental, though they may be added punctuation.

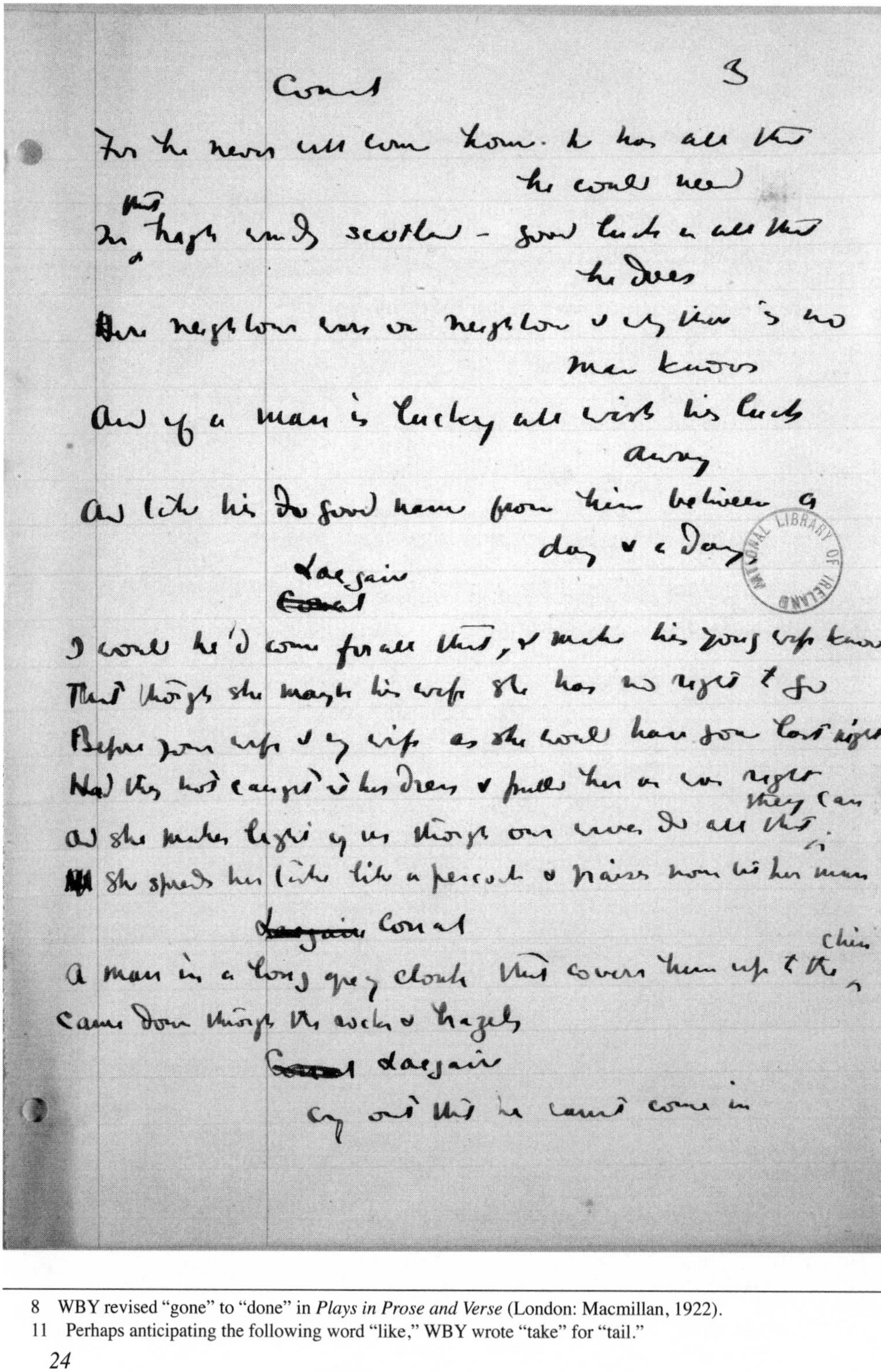
Conal 3

For he never will come home. he has all that he could need

In this high windy Scotland — good luck in all that he does

Here neighbour wars on neighbour & why there is no man knows

And if a man is lucky all wish his luck away

And take his good name from him between a day & a day

Laegaire
~~Conal~~

I would he'd come for all that, & make his young wife know

That though she may be his wife she has no right to go

Before your wife & my wife as she would have gone last night

Had they not caught at her dress & pulled her as was right

And she makes light of us though our wives do all that they can

~~Her~~ She spreads her take like a peacock & praises none but her man

~~Laegaire~~ Conal

A man in a long grey cloak that covers him up to the chin

Came down through the rocks & hazels

~~Conal~~ Laegaire

Cry out that he cannot come in

8 WBY revised "gone" to "done" in *Plays in Prose and Verse* (London: Macmillan, 1922).

11 Perhaps anticipating the following word "like," WBY wrote "take" for "tail."

[NLI 8761, 3[r]]

3

Conal [14–26]

1 For he never will come home. He has all that
he could need
that
2 In ^ high windy Scotland – good luck in all that
he does
3 Here neighbour wars on neighbour & why there is no
man knows
4 And if a man is lucky all wish his luck
away
5 And take his ~~de~~ good name from him between a
day & a day.

Laegaire
~~Conal~~
6 I would that he'd come for all that, & make his young wife know
7 That though she may be his wife she has not right to go
8 Before your wife & my wife as she would have [?g]one last night
9 Had they not caught at her dress & pulled her as was right
they can
10 And she makes light of us though our wives do all that ^
11 ~~[?And]~~ She spreads her take like a peacock and praises none but her man

~~Laegaire~~ Conal
chin
12 A man in a long grey cloak that covers him up to the ^
13 Came down through the rocks & hazels

~~Conal~~ Laegaire
14 Cry out that he cannot come in

---

1 home. He] home, he *Cuala*
2 does] does, *Cuala*
3 neighbour & why] neighbour and why *Cuala*
4 away] away, *Cuala*
5 day &] day and *Cuala*
6 would that he'd] would he'd *Cuala* that, &] that, and *Cuala*
7 wife she] wife, she *Cuala* not right] no right *Cuala*
8 wife & my wife] wife and my wife, *Cuala* [?g]one] gone *Cuala*
9 dress & pulled] dress, and pulled *Cuala* right] right; *Cuala*
10 can] can. *Cuala*
11 take] tail *Cuala* man] man.
12 grey] green *Cuala*
13 Came] Comes *Cuala* rocks & hazels] rocks and hazels, *Cuala*
14 come in] come in. *Cuala*

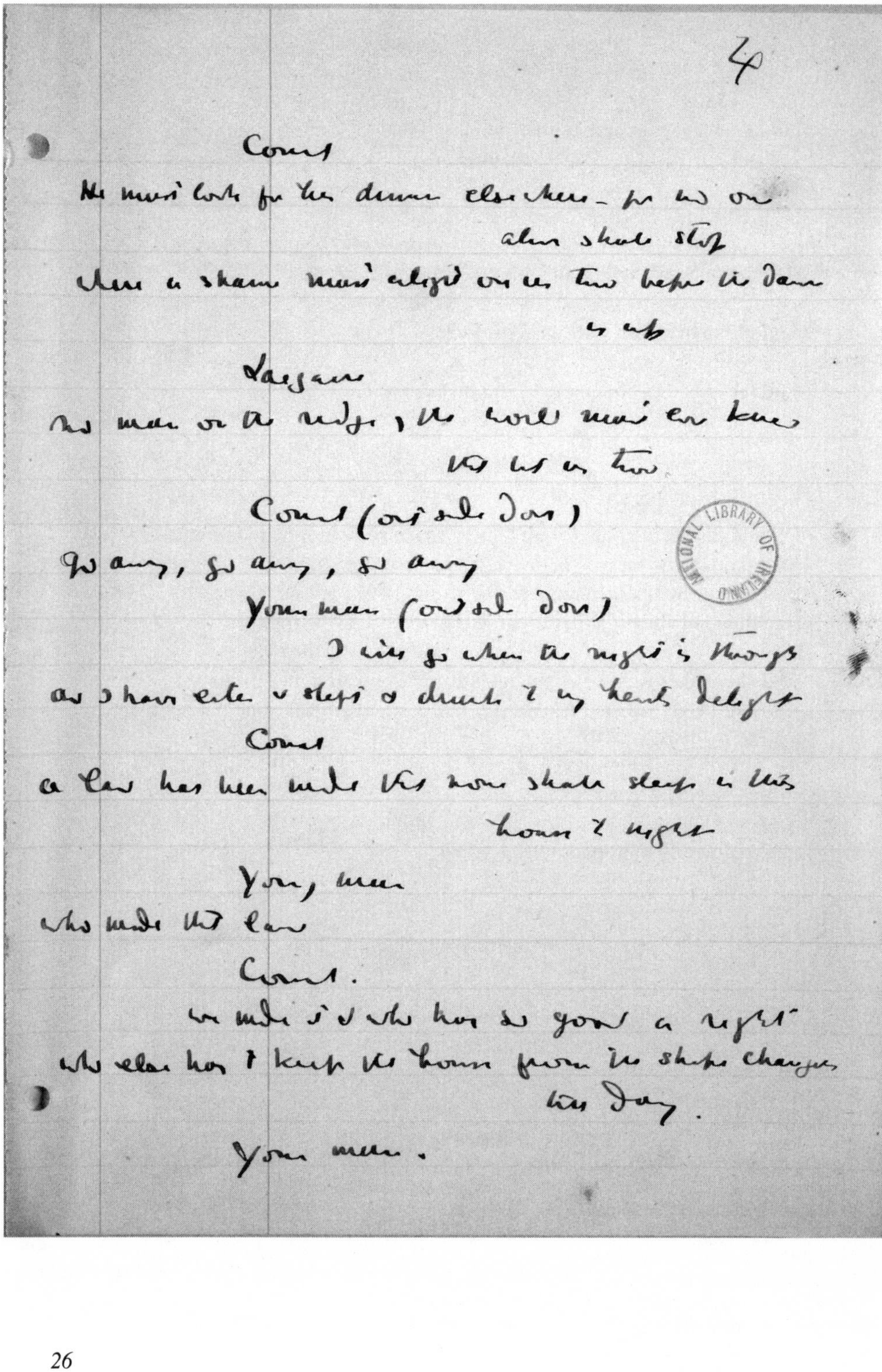
4

Count
He must look for his dinner elsewhere — for no one
alive shall stop
where a shame must alight on us two before the dawn
is up

Laegaire
No man on the ridge of the world must ever know
that but us two

Count (outside door)
Go away, go away, go away

Young man (outside door)
I will go when the night is through
and I have eaten & slept & drunk to my hearts delight

Count
A law has been made that none shall sleep in this
house to night

Young man
who made that law

Count.
We made it & who has so good a right
who else has to keep the house from the ship changes
this day.

Young man.

[NLI 8761, 4r]

4

Conal

1 He must look for his dinner else where – for no one alive shall stop [27–34]

2 Where a shame must alight on us two before the dawn is up

Laegaire

3 No man on the ridge of the world must ever know this but us two

Conal (outside door)

4 Go away, go away, go away

Young man (outside door)

5 I will go when the night is through

6 And I have eaten & slept & drunk to my hearts delight

Conal

7 A law has been made that none shall sleep in this house to night

Young man

8 Who made that law

Conal.

9 We made it & who has so good a right

10 Who else has to keep the house from the shape changers till day.

Young man.

---

1 else where –] elsewhere, *Cuala*
2 up] up. *Cuala*
3 this] that *Cuala* two] two. *Cuala*
4 go away, go away] go away, go away. *Cuala*
6 eaten & slept & drunk] eaten and slept and drunk *Cuala* hearts delight] heart's delight. *Cuala*
7 to night] to-night. *Cuala*
8 law] law? *Cuala*
9 made it &] made it, and *Cuala*
10 shape changers] Shape-Changers *Cuala* day.] day? *Cuala*

5

Then I will unmake the law & get you out of the way
(He pushes past Conall & goes in to the house)

Conall

I thought that no man ~~then~~ living could have
pushed me from the door
nor could any living man do it but for the dip in the floor
And had I been rightly ready theres no man living could do it
Dip or no dip.

~~Young man.~~

Laegaire

Go out — if you have your wits about
a stones throw further on — you will find a big house where
our master will give you supper & you'll sleep soundly
there
For its a luckier house

Young man,

I'll eat & sleep where I will

Laegaire

Go out or I will make you.

Young man (forcing up Laegaires arm
passing him & putting his shield on the wall over
the chair) not till I have drunk my fill
But Connaught cat defend me for a dog of wonders up

[NLI 8761, 5^{r}]

5

Then I will unmake the law so get you out of the way [35–44]
(He pushes past Conal & goes into house)

Conal
I thought that no man ~~alive~~ living could have
pushed me from the door
And could any living man do it but for the dip in the floor
And had I been rightly ready theres no man living could do it
Dip or no dip.

~~Young man.~~
Laegaire
Go out – if you have your wits do out
A stone's throw further on – you will find a big house where
Our wives will give you supper & you'll sleep sounder
there
For its a luckier house

Young man.
I'll eat & sleep where I will

Laegaire
Go out or I will make you.

Young man (forcing up Laegaires arm
passing him & putting his shield on the wall over
the chair) Not till I have drunk my fill
But Connaght cats defend me for a dog of wonders up

---

1 law so] law, so *Cuala* way] way. *Cuala*
1*sd* & goes] and goes *Cuala*
2 no man living] no living man *Cuala*
3 and could] Nor could *Cuala* floor] floor;
4 theres] there's *Cuala* do it] do it, *Cuala*
6 wits do out] wits, go out, *Cuala*
7 further on – you] further on you *Cuala*
8 supper & you'll] supper, and you'll *Cuala* there] there, *Cuala*
9 its] it's *Cuala* house] house. *Cuala*
10 eat & sleep] eat and sleep *Cuala* will] will. *Cuala*
12*sd* Legaires] Legaire's *Cuala*
12 fill] fill, *Cuala*
13 Connaught cats defend] may some dog defend *Cuala* dog of wonders up] cat of wonders up. *Cuala*

---

6 For "do out" read "go out."

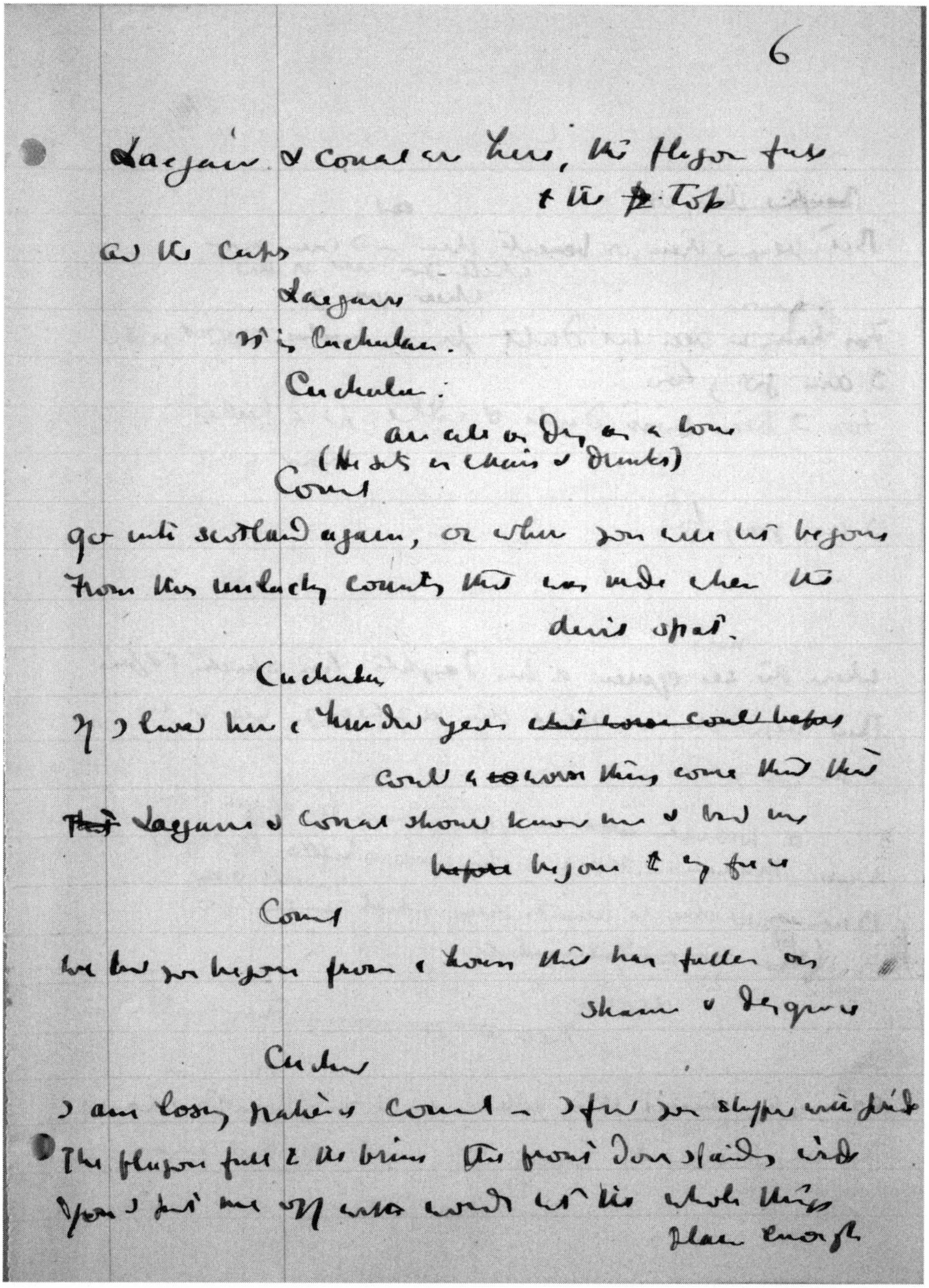

6

Laegaire & Conal are here, the flagon full
& the ~~[?]~~ top

at the cups

Laegaire

It is Cuchulain.

Cuchulain:

an ale or dy or a horn
(He sits in chair & drinks)

Conal

go into Scotland again, or where you will but begone
From this unlucky country that was made when the
devil spat.

Cuchulain

If I live here a hundred years ~~that some could before~~
could a ~~[?]~~ worse thing come than that
~~That~~ Laegaire & Conal should know me & bid me
~~before~~ begone to my face

Conal

We bid you begone from a house that has fallen on
shame & disgrace

Cuchulain

I am losing patience Conal — I find you stupid with drink
The flagon full to the brim the front door standing wide
You put me off with words but the whole thing's
plain enough

[NLI 8761, 6^{r}]

6

1 Laegaire & Conal are here, the flagon full [45–54]
to the ~~to~~ top
2 And the cups

Laegaire
3 It is Cuchulain.

Cuchulain
4 Are all dry as a bone
(He sits on chair & drinks)

Conal
5 Go into Scotland again, or where you will but begone
6 From this unlucky country that was made when the
devil spat.

Cuchulain
7 If I lived here a hundred years ~~what worse could befall~~
could a ~~w~~ worse thing come than that
8 ~~That~~ Leagarie & Conal should know me & bid me
~~before~~ begone to my face

Conal
9 We bid you begone from a house that has fallen on
shame & disgrace

Cuchulain
10 I am losing patience Conal – I find you stuffed with pride
11 The flagon full to the brim the front door standing wide
12 You d put me off with words but the whole things
plain enough

---

1 & Conal] and Conall *Cuala* the top] the top,
2 cups] cups. *Cuala*
4 Are all dry as a bone] The cups are dry as a bone. *Cuala*
5 will but] will, but *Cuala*
7 years could] years, could *Cuala* that that] than that, *Cuala*
8 me & bid] me and bid *Cuala* face] face? *Cuala*
9 shame & disgrace] shame and disgrace. *Cuala*
10 patience Conal] patience, Conall *Cuala* pride] pride, *Cuala*
11 brim the] brim, the *Cuala* wide] wide; *Cuala*
12 words but] words, but *Cuala* enough] enough, *Cuala*

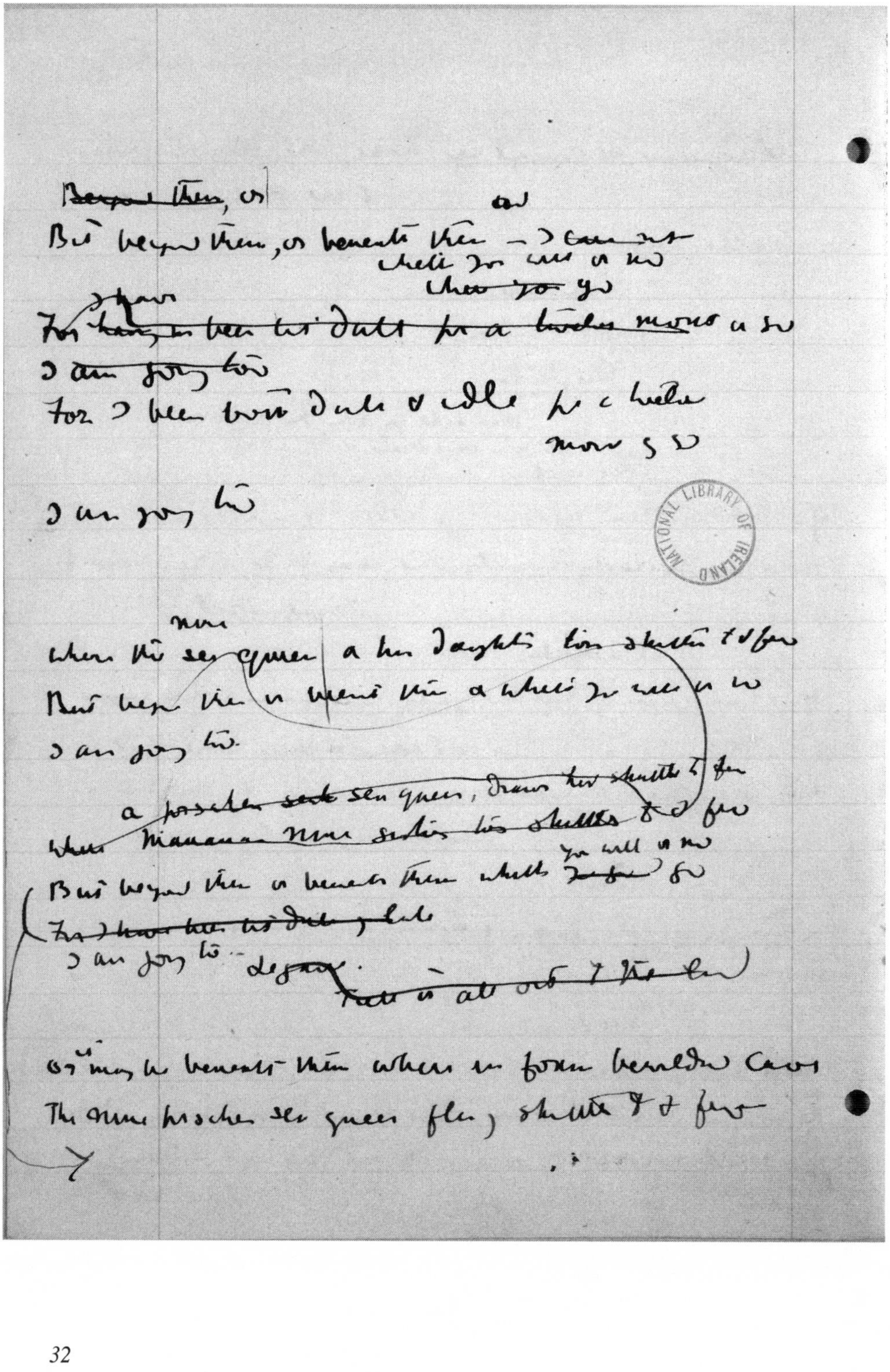

[NLI 8761, 6[v]]

~~Beyond them~~, or and
1 But beyond them, or beneath them – I ~~care not~~ [56–60]
whether you will or no
~~where you go~~

~~I have~~
~~For having [?be] been but dull for a twelve month or so~~
~~I am going too~~
2 For I have been both dull & idle for a twelve
month or so
3 I am going too

nine
4 Where the sea queen & her daughters toss shuttles to & fro

5 But beyon them or beneat them & wheth yo will or no
6 I am going too
a forsaken seek sea queen, draws her shuttle to fro
7 Where Mananans nine sisters toss shuttles to & fro
you will or no[?t]
8 But beyond them or beneath them whethr ~~you go~~ go
9 ~~For I have been but dull of late~~
10 I am going to . –

~~Leagaire~~.
11 ~~Tell it all out to the end~~
it
12 Or may be beneath them where in foam bewildered caves
13 The nine forsaken sea queens fling shuttles to & fro

On 6[v] WBY attempted several alternate versions of ll. 1–6 on the facing page, 7[r]. The final version here, ll. 8–13 as revised, appears in *Cuala*. See the collations on p. 35, below.

5 The number of incomplete words attest to the speed with which WBY composed this passage.

[NLI 8761, 7r]

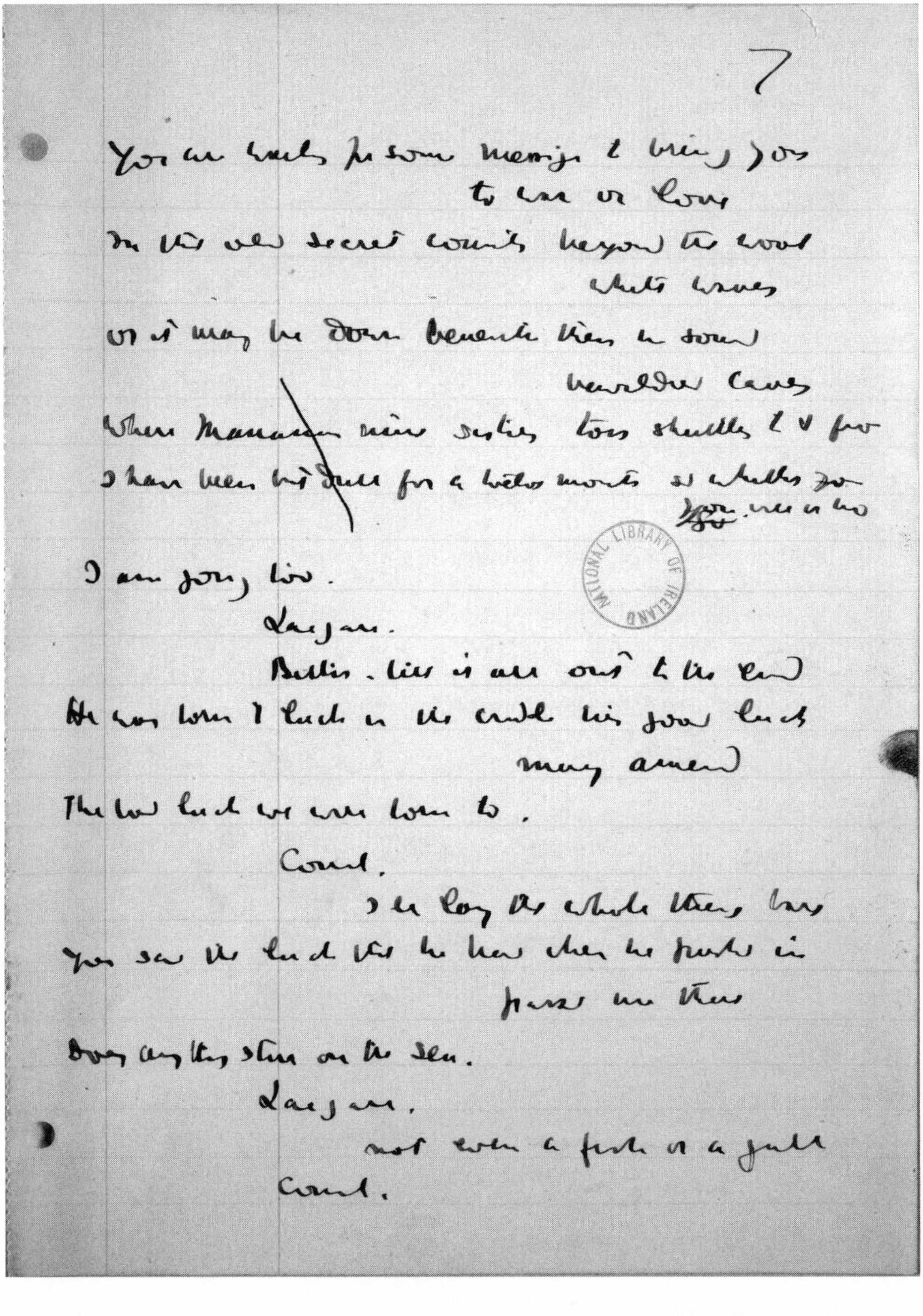
7

You are waiting for some message to bring you
to war or love
In this old secret country beyond the wool
white waves
Or it may be down beneath them in some
wave-worn caves
Where Manannan's nine sisters toss shuttles to & fro
I have been but dull for a twelve month at whatever ~~you~~
~~you~~ were in [illegible]

I am going too.

Laegaire.

Better this is all out to the end
He was born to luck in the cradle his good luck
may amend
The bad luck we were born to.

Conall.

I'll lay the whole thing bare
You saw the luck that he had when he parted in
passed me there
Does anything stir on the sea.

Laegaire.

not even a fish or a gull

Conall.

[NLI 8761, 7r]

7

1 You are waiting for some message to bring you [55–64]
to war or love
2 In the old secret country beyond the wool
white waves
3 Or it may be down beneath them in foam
bewildered caves
4 Where Manannans nine sisters toss shuttles to & fro
5 I have been but dull for a twelve month so whether ~~yo~~
you will or no
~~go~~
6 I am going too.

Laegaire.

7 Better tell it all out to the end
8 He was born to luck in the cradle his good luck
9 may amend
10 The bad luck we were born to.

Conal.

11 I ll lay the whole thing bare
12 You saw the luck that he had when he pushed in
past me there
13 Does anything stir on the sea.

Laegaire.

14 Not even a fish or a gull

Conal.

---

2 In the] In that *Cuala* wool white waves] wool-white waves, *Cuala*
3 foam bewildered] foam-bewildered *Cuala*
4 Where Manannans nine sisters toss] Where nine forsaken sea queens fling *Cuala* fro] fro; *Cuala*
5 I have been but dull for a twelve month so whether you will or no] But beyond them, or beneath them, whether you will or no, *Cuala*
6 too] too.
7 end] end; *Cuala*
8 cradle his] cradle, his *Cuala*
11 I ll] I'll *Cuala* bare] bare. *Cuala*
12 there] there. *Cuala*
13 sea.] sea? *Cuala*
14 gull] gull. *Cuala*

8

You were gone but a little while we were there &
the wine cups full
we were half drunk & merry & midnight on the stroke
When a middle high man came in with a red foxy cloak
with half shut foxy eyes & a great laughing mouth
~~and all the waves of the sea had not appeased his drouth~~
And he said when we had been drunk that he had so
great a drouth
he could drink up the sea.

Cuchullain.

~~And I~~ thought him a cunning cat.

~~That comely man was he & made it by this you worse than this~~
~~For when we had sung & danced as he was our next of kin~~
~~He said he would show us a game the best that could have been.~~

I thought he'd come by from you
out of some cunning witch & that I'd have him near
but if he so loved water ~~I shall~~ I have the tide [illegible].

You would ~~[illegible]~~ not be so merry comes at them if he were standing by
For when we had sung & danced as he ~~were~~ our
next of kin

[NLI 8761, 8r]

8

1 You were gone but a little while we were there & [65–74]
the wine cup full
2 We were half drunk & merry & midnight on the stroke
3 When a wide high man came in with a red foxy cloke
4 With half shut foxy eyes & a great laughing mouth
~~And all the waves of the sea had not [?appesd]~~ his
~~drout~~
5 And he said when we bid him drink that he had so
great a drout
6 He could drink up the sea.

Cuchulain
~~And I thought~~ him a Connaught cat.

Conal
a thing
That too was ^ bad ^ to mock it but this was worse than that
For when we had sung & danced as he was our next of kin
been
He said he would show us a game the best that ever had ^
for
7 I thought he d come ~~to~~ you
8 Out of some Connagh rath & think I hear him mew
9 But if he so loved water ~~I shall~~ I have the tale arie.

Conal
not be so merry
10 You would ~~not mock at him~~ if he were standing by
11 For when we had sung or danced as he were our
next of kin

---

1 while we] while. We *Cuala* there & the wine cup full] there and the ale-cup full. *Cuala*
2 drunk & merry & midnight] drunk and merry, and midnight *Cuala*
3 cloke] cloak, *Cuala*
4 eyes &] eyes and *Cuala* mouth] mouth, *Cuala*
5 drink that] drink, that *Cuala* drout] drouth *Cuala*
6 drink up] drink *Cuala*
7 thought he d come for you] thought he had come for one of you *Cuala*
8 Connagh rath & think I hear him mew] Connaught rath, and would lap up milk and mew. *Cuala*
9 arie] awry *Cuala*
10 standing by] standing by, *Cuala*

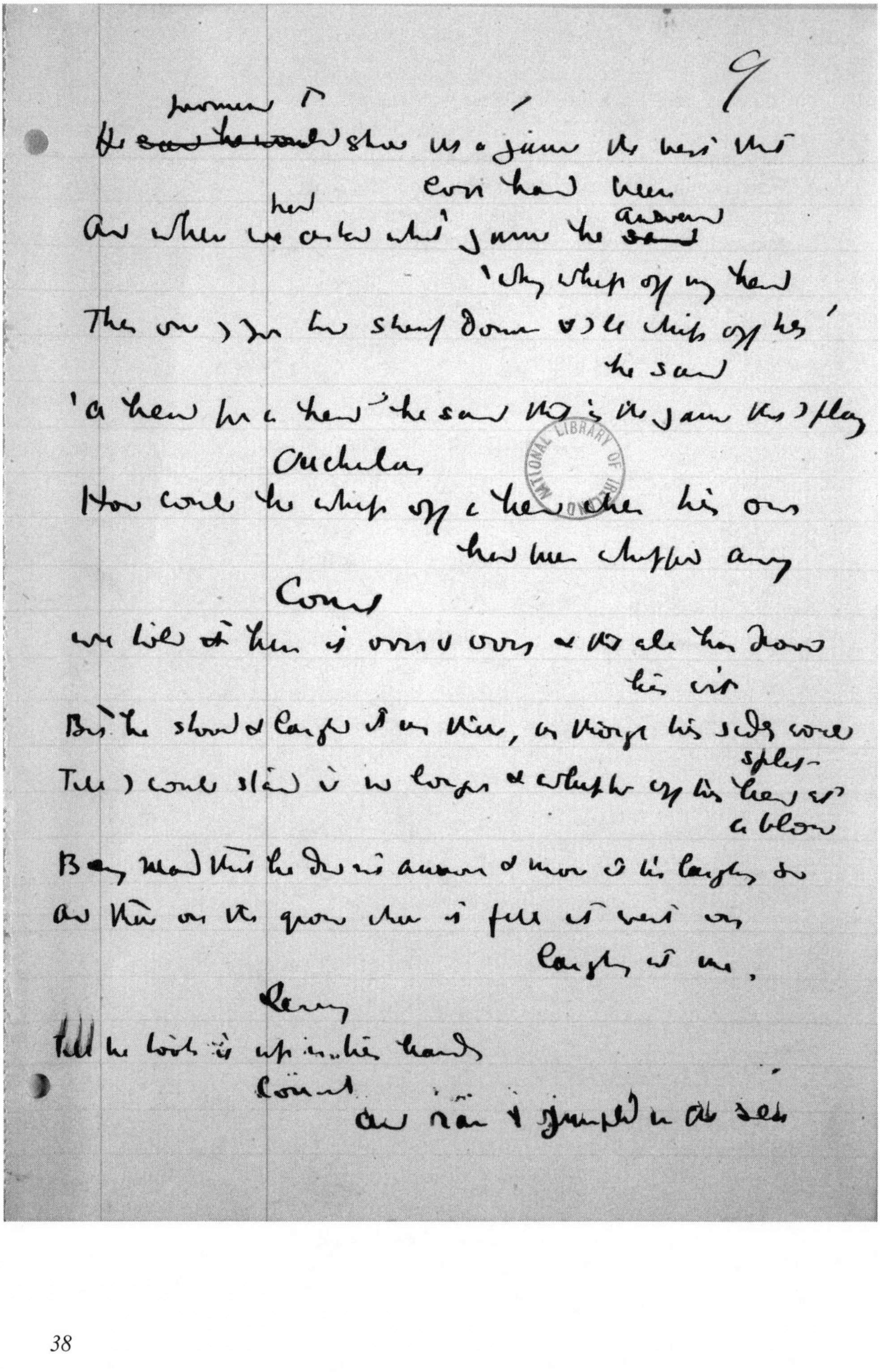
9

promised to
He [illegible] showed us a game the best that ever had been
And when we asked what game he answered
'whip off my head
Then one of you stoop down and I'll whip off his'
he said
'A head for a head' he said 'that is the game that I play'
Aechulain
How could he whip off a head when his own
had been chopped away
Conall
We told it him in over & over & that ale had drowned
his wit
But he shouted & laughed at us then, as though his sides would split
Till I could stand it no longer & whipped off his head at a blow
Being mad that he did not answer & more at his laughing so
And there on the ground where it fell it went on
laughing at me.
Leary
Till he took it up in his hands
Conall
And ran & jumped in the sea

[NLI 8761, 9r]

9

promised to
1 He ~~said he would~~ show us a game the best that [75–85]
ever had been
had answered
2 And when we asked what game he ~~said~~
'why whip off my head
3 Then one of you two stoop down & I'll whip off his'
he said
4 'A head for a head' he said that is the game that I play

Cuchulain
5 How could he whip off a head when his own
had been whipped away

Conal
6 We told ~~it~~ him it over & over & that ale had drowned
his wit
7 But he stood & laughed at us there, as though his sides would
split
8 Till I could stand it no longer & whipped off his head at
a blow
9 Being mad that he did not answer & more at his laughing so
10 And there on the ground where it fell it went on
laughing at me.

Leary
11 Till he took it up in his hands

Conal
12 And ran & jumped in the sea

---

1 game the] game, the *Cuala* been] been; *Cuala*
2 what game he answered] what game, he answered, *Cuala* head] head, *Cuala*
3 down & I'll] down and I'll *Cuala* his'] his,' *Cuala* said] said. *Cuala*
4 for a head'] for a head,' *Cuala* he said that is the game that I play] he said, 'that is the game that I play.' *Cuala*
5 away] away? *Cuala*
6 over & over &] over and over, and *Cuala* drowned] fuddled *Cuala* wit] wit, *Cuala*
7 stood & laughed] stood and laughed *Cuala*
8 longer & whipped] longer, and whipped *Cuala* blow] blow, *Cuala*
9 answer &] answer, and *Cuala* so] so, *Cuala*
11 Leary *rev to* Laegaire *Cuala* hands] hands. *Cuala*
12 ran & jumped in] splashed himself into *Cuala* sea] sea. *Cuala*

[NLI 8761, 10r]

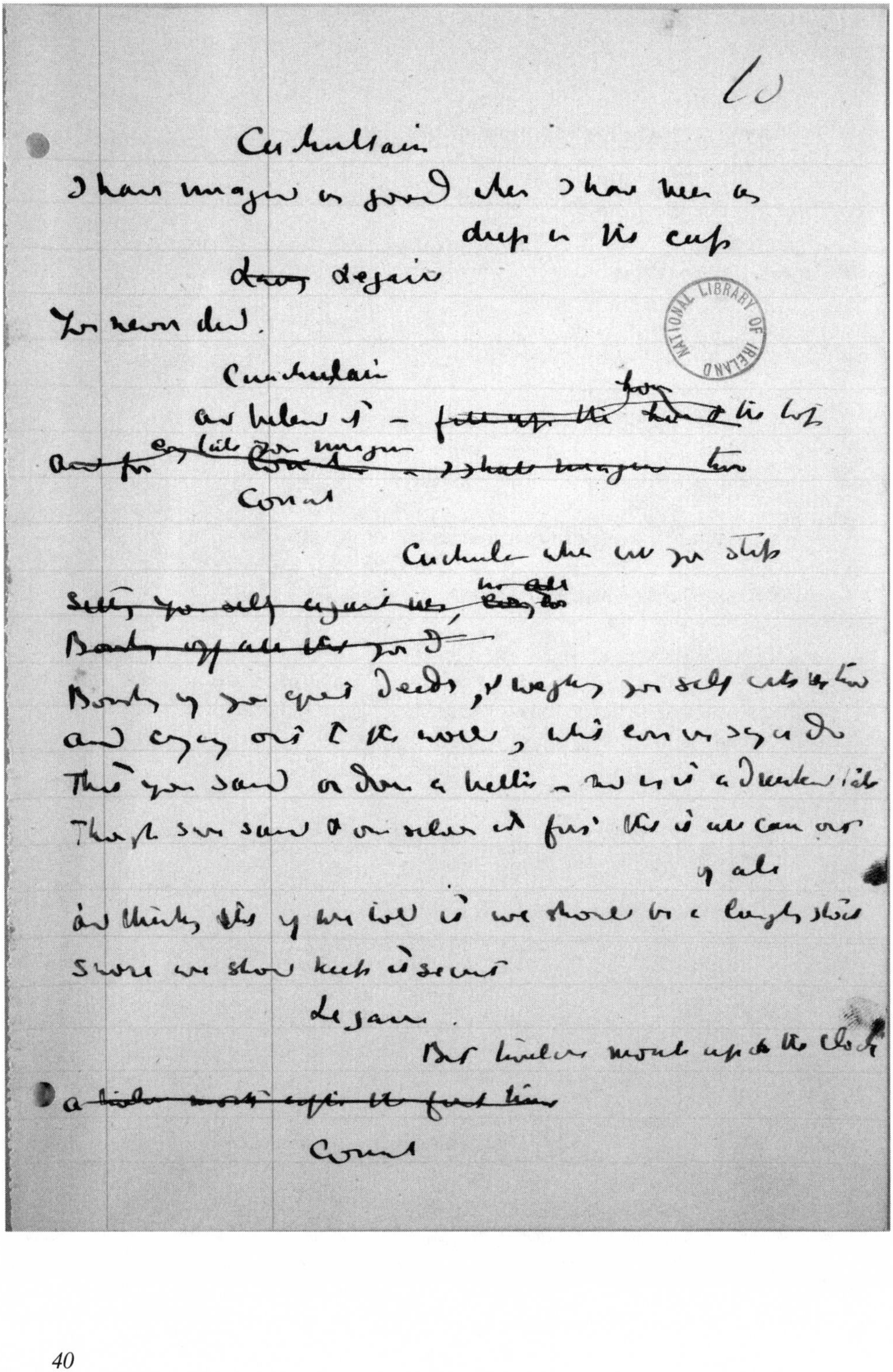
10

Cuchulain

I have imagined as good ales I have seen as
deep in the cup

~~Laery~~ Legaire

You never did.

Cuchulain

As I believe it — ~~[illegible]~~ [illegible]

~~And for~~ [illegible] ~~[illegible]~~

Conal

Cuchulain when will you stop

~~Setting your self against us, [illegible]~~

~~Boasting [illegible]~~

Boasting of your great deeds, & weighing your self [illegible]

and crying out to the world, [illegible]

[illegible]

[illegible]

[illegible]

Swore we should keep it secret

Legaire

But [illegible]

~~a [illegible]~~

Conal

[NLI 8761, 10r]

10

Cuchullain

1 I have imagined as good when I have been as [86–93]

deep in the cup

~~Laeg~~ Legaire

2 You never did.

Cuchulain

~~horn~~

3 And believed it – ~~fill up the horn to the top~~

~~every tale you imagine~~

4 ~~And for – I shall imagine two~~

~~Conal.~~

Conal

5 Cuchulan when will you stop

us all

Setting your self against us, ~~every [?one/man]~~

Boasting off all that you d

6 Boasting of your great deeds & weighing yourself with us two
7 And crying out to the world, whatever we say or do
8 That you said or done a better – nor is it a drunkard tale
9 Though we said to ourselves at first that it all came out

of ale

10 And thinking that if we told it we should be a laughing stock
11 Swore we should keep it secret

Legaire.

12 But twelve monts upon the clock

~~a twelve month after the first time~~

Conal

---

1 cup] cup. *Cuala*
3 believed it –] believed it. *Cuala*
5 Cuchulan when] Cuchulain, when *Cuala*
6 deeds & weighing] deeds, and weighing *Cuala* two] two, *Cuala*
7 world, whatever] world whatever *Cuala* do] do, *Cuala*
8 you said] you have said *Cuala* drunkard tale] drunkard's tale? *Cuala*
9 ale] ale, *Cuala*
11 secret] secret. *Cuala*
12 monts upon the clock] months upon the clock. *Cuala*

3–4 After entering the part ascription for Conall, WBY canceled it and squeezed the continuation of l. 3 around it. He then struck out the added words.

11

A twelve month from the first time,

Legaire,

And the jug full up to the brim

For we had been ~~put~~ put from our drinking by the very
thoughts of him

~~Though we thought ... that~~
~~After we thought his nothing~~, Conal —
We stood on our legs now

Legaire.

The horn was ~~all~~ as empty

Conal

He ran out, and then with his head on his
shoulder again.

Cuchulain

Why this is a tale worth telling.

Conal.

And he called for his debt & his rights ~~and his rights~~ ~~for the head that was due~~
And said that this land was disgraced, because of us him from
the right
if we did not pay him his debt.

Legaire

What is there to be said

[NLI 8761, 11^{r}]

11

A twelve mont[?h] from the first time, [94–100]

Legaire.

And the jug full up to the brim

For we had been ~~but~~ put from our drinking by the mere

thought of him

~~Though we thought him but a [?tale]~~

~~After we thought him nothing.~~

Conal –

We stood as we're standing now

Legaire.

as

The horns were ~~all~~ empty

Conal

When

He ran up out of the sea with his head on his

shoulders again.

Cuchulain

Why then its a tale worth telling.

Conal.

for his debt & his right

~~out his right~~

And he called ^ ~~for the head that was due~~

And said that the land was disgraced, because of us two from

that night

If we did not pay him his debt.

Legaire.

What is there to be said

---

1 time,] time. *Cuala*
2 brim] brim. *Cuala*
3 mere] very *Cuala* him] him. *Cuala*
4 now] now. *Cuala*
5 empty] empty. *Cuala*
8 Why then its] Why, this is *Cuala*
9 debt & his] debt and his *Cuala*
10 night] night, *Cuala*

The canceled lines after l. 3 were squeezed in after the part ascription and speech for Conall were entered.

[NLI 8761, 12r]

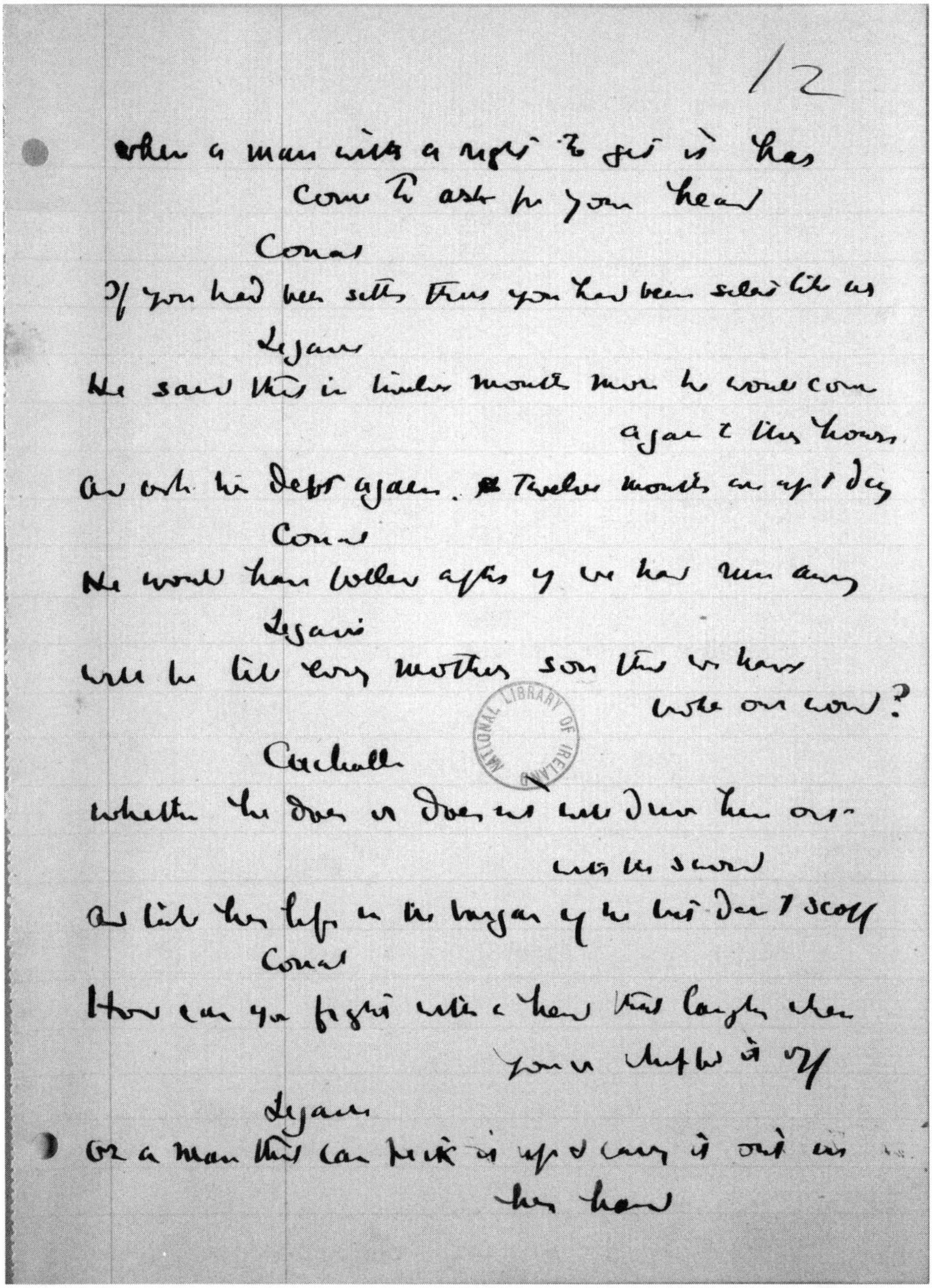

12

when a man with a right to get it has
come to ask for your head

Conal

If you had been sitting there you had been silent like us

Laegaire

He said that in twelve months more he would come
again to this house
And ask his debt again. Twelve months and a day

Conal

He would have walked after if we had run away

Laegaire

Will he tell every mother's son that we have
broke our word?

Cuchullain

Whether he does or does not we'll drive him out
with the sword
And take his life in the bargain if he but dare to scoff

Conal

How can you fight with a head that laughs when
you've chopped it off

Laegaire

Or a man that can pick it up and carry it out in
his hand

[NLI 8761, 12^{r}]

12

1 When a man with a right to get it has
come to ask for your head [101–110]

Conal

2 If you had been sitting there you had been silent like us

Legarie

3 He said that in twelve months more he would come
again to this house

4 And ask his debt again. & Twelve months are up today

Conal

5 He would have followed after if we had run away

Leagaire

6 Will he tell every mothers son that we have
broke our word?

Cuchulain

7 Whether he does or does not well drive him out
with the sword

8 And take his life in the bargain if he but dare to scoff

Conal

9 How can you fight with a head that laughs when
you ve whipped it off

Legaire

10 Or a man that can pick it up & carry it out in
his hand

---

1 head] head? *Cuala*
2 us] us. *Cuala*
4 today] to-day. *Cuala*
5 away] away. *Cuala*
6 mothers] mother's *Cuala* broke] broken *Cuala*
7 well] we'll *Cuala* sword] sword, *Cuala*
8 scoff] scoff. *Cuala*
9 you ve] you've *Cuala* off] off? *Cuala*
10 up & carry] up and carry *Cuala* hand] hand? *Cuala*

[NLI 8761, 13r]

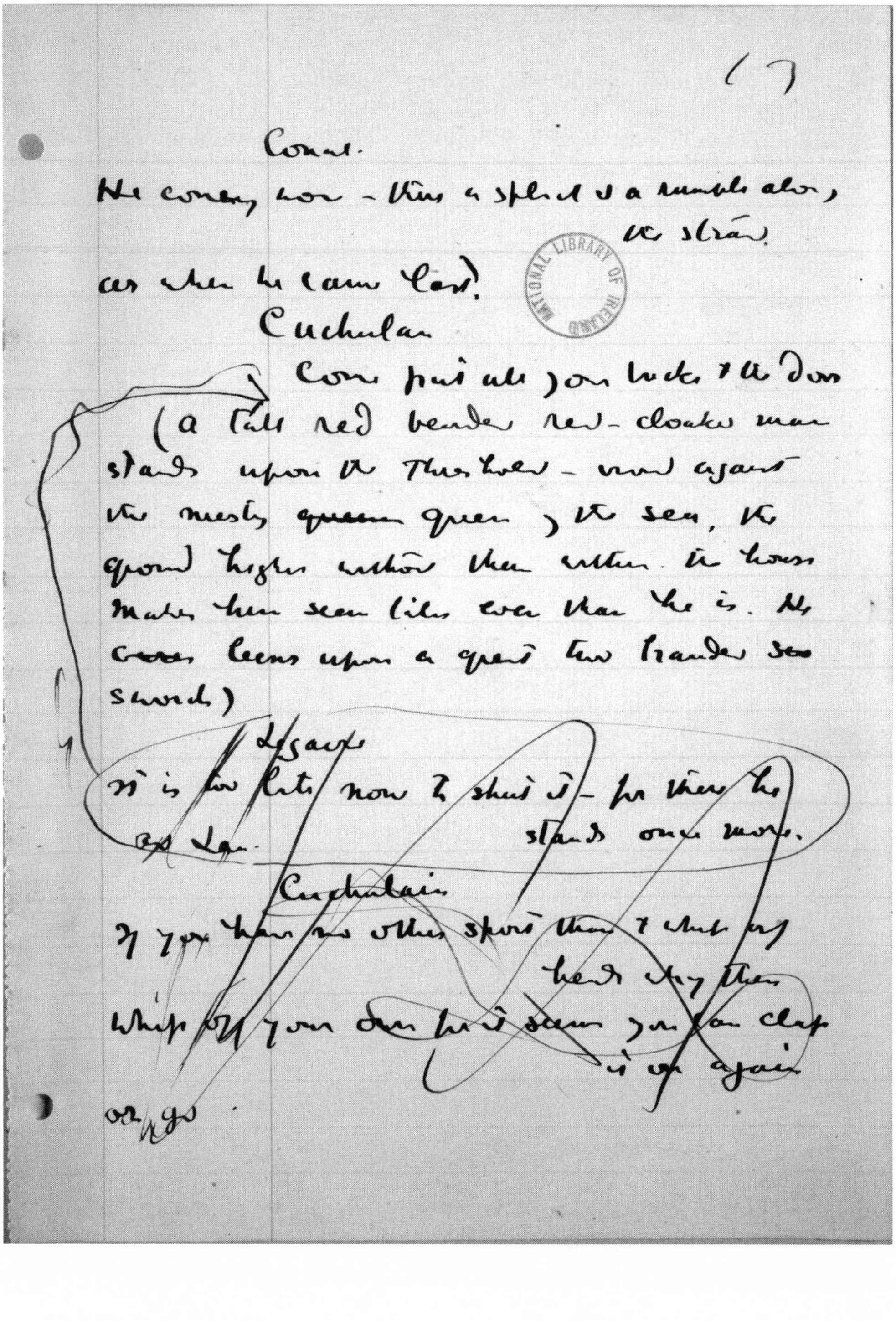
(7)

Conal.

He coming now – there's a splash and a tumble along the strand

as when he came last.

Cuchulain

Come put all your backs to the door

(a tall red bearded red-cloaked man stands upon the threshold – vivid against the misty queen green of the sea, the ground higher without than within the house makes him seem taller even than he is. He leans upon a great two handed sword.)

Laegaire

It is too late now to shut it – for there he stands once more.

as I am.

Cuchulain

If you have no other sport than to cut off heads, why then whip off your own head seeing you can clap it on again

or go.

[NLI 8761, 13r]

13

Conal

1 He coming now – theres a splash & a rumble along
the strand [111–116]

2 As when he came last.

Cuchulain

3 Come put all your backs t th door

(a tall red bearded red-cloaked man
stands upon the threshold – now against
the misty ~~green~~ green of the sea, the
ground higher without than within the house
makes him seem taler even than he is. He
~~car[?i]es~~ leens upon a great two handed ~~sw~~
sword)

Legaire

4 It is too late now to shut it – for there he
stands once more.

5 And La.

Cuchulain

6 If you have no other sport than to whip off
heads why then

7 Whip off your own for it seems you can clap
it on again

8 Or go

---

1 He coming now –] He is coming now, *Cuala* splash &] splash and *Cuala*

3 Come put] Come, and put *Cuala* t th door] to the door. *Cuala*

3*sd* red bearded] red-headed *Cuala* threshold – now against] threshold against *Cuala* leens] leans *Cuala* two handed] two-handled *Cuala*

4 shut it –] shut it, *Cuala* more.] more *Cuala*

5 And La.] And laughs like the sea. *Cuala*

---

sd WBY restored the reading "two-handed" in the Shakespeare Head Press edition *The Green Helmet, An Heroic Farce* in 1911 (Wade 89).

5 The words "And La" are an aborted start of the line "And laughs like the sea."

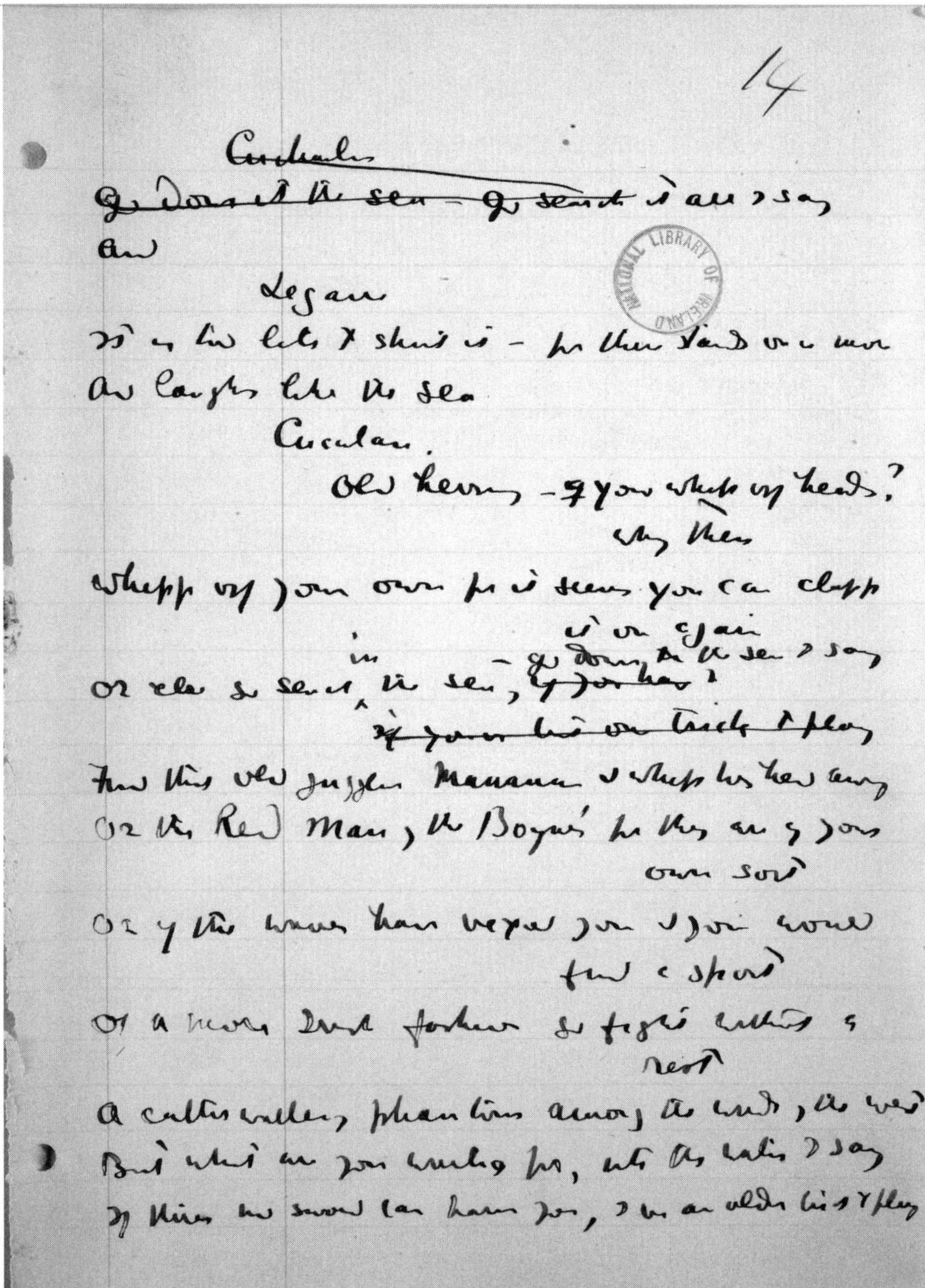
14

Conall

~~Go down to the sea — go search~~ it all I say

Emer

Legaire

It is the lot of such as — for they stand on a moor

And laughs like the sea

Cuchulain.

Old herring — ~~if~~ you whip up heads?

why then

Whip up your own for it seems you can clap

it on again

in — go down to the sea I say

Or else go search, the sea, ~~if you have~~?

~~If you are used to tricks & play~~

From this old juggler Manannan I whip his head away

Or the Red Man, the Boyne's for they are of your

own sort

Or if the waves have vexed you & you would

find a sport

Of a more dread fashion go fight with the

rest

A cattle-walker, phantoms among the winds, the west

But what are you waiting for, with the ladies I say

If there be no sword can harm you, I'm an older [illegible] play

[NLI 8761, 14r]

14

G} ~~Cuchulain~~
~~g }o down to the sea – go search it all I say~~
And

Legaire
Is it too late to shut it – for there he stands once more [113–123]
And laughs like the sea

Cuculain.
Old herring – ~~y~~ you whip off heads?
Why then
Whipp off your own for it seems you can clapp
it on again
in – go down to the sea I say
Or else go search ^ the sea, ~~if you hav~~
~~if you've but one trick to play~~
Find that old juggler Manann & whip his head away
Or the Red Man of the Boyne's for they are of your
own sort
Or if the waves have vexed you & you would
find a sport
Of a more Irish fashion go fight without a
rest
A catterwalling phantom among the winds of the west
But what are you waiting for, into the water I say
If theres no sword can harm you, I ve an older trick to play

---

3 shut it – for] shut it, for *Cuala*
4 sea] sea. *Cuala*
5 you] You *Cuala*
6 Whipp] Whip *Cuala* own for] own, for *Cuala* again] again. *Cuala*
7 Or else go down in the sea, go down in the sea I say, *Cuala*
8 Manann & whip] Manannan and whip *Cuala* away] away; *Cuala*
9 Boyne's] Boynes' *Cuala* sort] sort, *Cuala*
10 you &] you and *Cuala*
11 fashion go] fashion, go *Cuala*
12 catterwalling] caterwauling *Cuala* west] west. *Cuala*
13 say] say? *Cuala*
14 theres] there's *Cuala* I ve] I've *Cuala* play] play, *Cuala*

65

An old fear finger trick to tumble you over
of the floor

~~sweets of hands on your shoulders all tumble~~ you
out the door

~~I am Cuchulain, son of Sualam~~

I am Sualtim's son Cuchulain — ~~what do you laugh at me~~.
what do you laugh in my face?

Red Man.

So you think me in earnest in anger, but for but
a drunken joker a gibe & a ~~juggler~~ juggler for this is all
To make the time go quickly — for I am the drunken fiend
The kindest of all shape changers from here to the
worlds end
The best of all tipsy comrades & now I bring you a
gift
I will lay it there on the ground for the best of
you all to lift.

(He lays his Helmet on the ground)

And wear upon his own head, & choose for yourselves
the best.

O Legaire & Conal are brave but they were afraid of
my jest.

Well maybe I jest the greatest when the ale is in the cup
There I am forgiven now — (then in a more
solemn voice as he goes out)
Let the bravest take it up.

[NLI 8761, 15[r]]

15

to
1 An old five fingered trick ~~&~~ tumble you out of the place [124–135]
~~As with my hands on your shoulders I'll tumble you~~ into the sea
~~I am Cuchulan, son of Sualam~~
2 I am Sualtim s son Cuchulln – ~~what do you laugh at me~~. What do you laugh in my face?

Red Man.
3 So you t think me in earnest in wagering pol for pol
4 A drinking joke & a gibe & a ~~jug~~ jugglers feat that is all
for
5 To make the time go quickly – ~~as~~ ^ I am the drinkers friend
6 The kindest of all shape changers from here to the E} worlds e ∫nd
7 The best of all tipsey comrades & now I bring you a gift
8 I will lay it there on the ground for the best of you all to lift –
(He lays his Helmet on the ground)
9 And wear upon his own head; & choose for your selves the best.
10 O Legaire & Conal are brave but they were afraid of my jest.
11 Well maybe I jest too grimly when the ale is in the cup
12 There I m forgiven now – (then in a more solemn voice as he goes out) Let the bravest take it up.

---

1 five fingered] five-fingered *Cuala* place] place; *Cuala*
2 Sualtim s son Cuchulln—What do] Sualtim's son Cuchulain—What, do *Cuala*
3 t think] too think *Cuala* in wagering pol for pol] is wagering poll for poll, *Cuala*
4 gibe & a jugglers] gibe and a juggler's *Cuala* all] all, *Cuala*
5 drinkers friend] drinker's friend, *Cuala*
6 shape changers] Shape-Changers *Cuala* worlds End] world's end. *Cuala*
7 tipsey comrades & now] tipsy companions, and now *Cuala* gift] gift, *Cuala*
8 lift –] lift, *Cuala*
8*sd* He] he *Cuala* Helmet] helmet *Cuala*
9 head; &] head, and *Cuala* your selves] yourselves *Cuala*
10 O Legaire & Conal] O! Leagaire and Conall *Cuala* brave but] brave, but *Cuala*
11 Well maybe] Well, maybe *Cuala* cup] cup. *Cuala*
12 There I m forgiven] There, I'm forgiven *Cuala*

---

3 The *Cuala* printer's error—"is wagering"—was corrected to "in wagering" in 1911.

[NLI 8761, 16r]

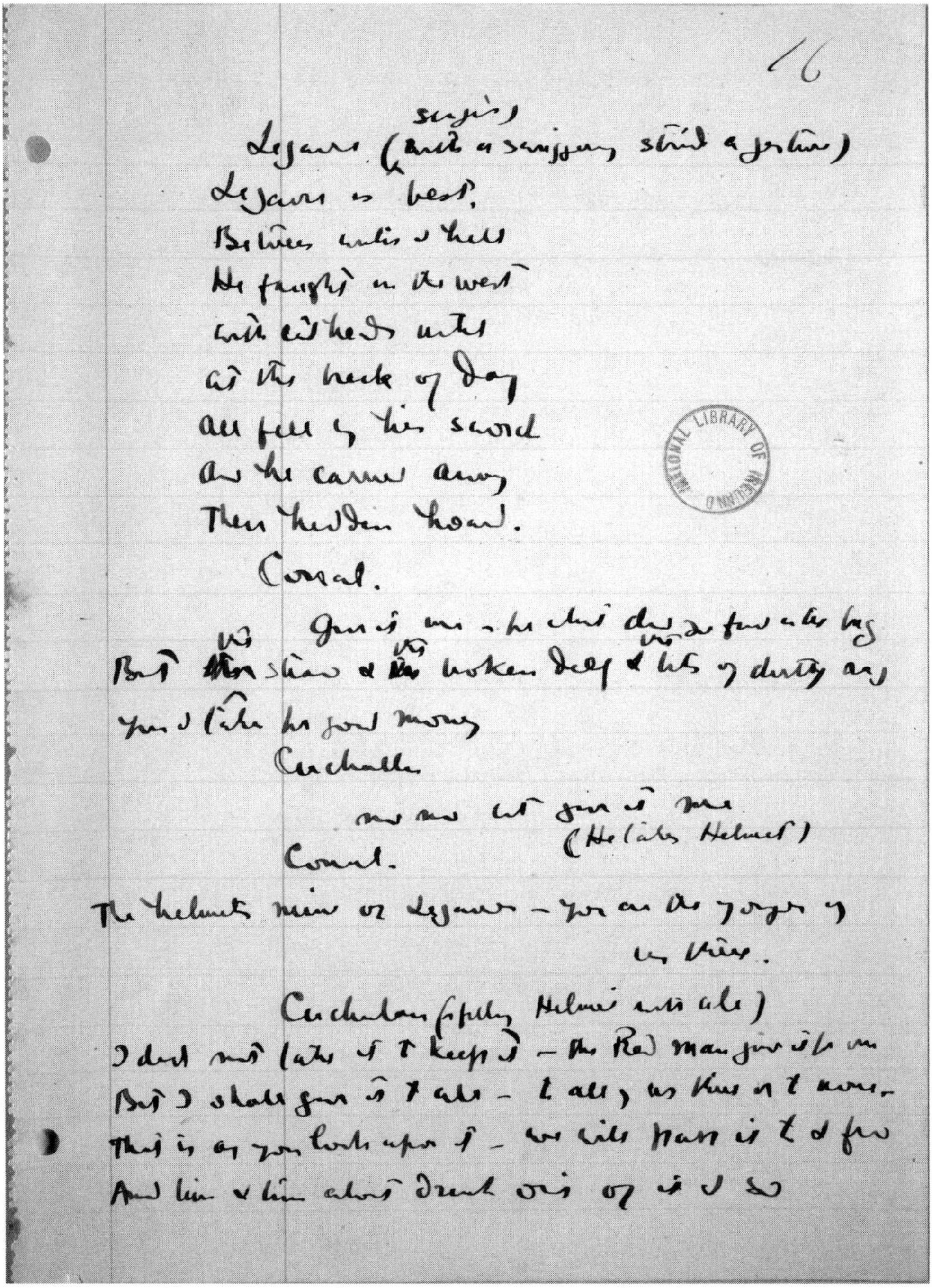

16

Leagerie (with a swaggering stride & gesture) singing)

Leagerie is best.

Between white & hell

He fought in the west

With cut heads until

At the break of day

All fell by his sword

And he carried away

Their hidden hoard.

Conal.

Give it me — he that drew the fine white bag

But the straw & the broken delf & bits of dirty rags

Would take his good money

Cuchulain

No no let give it me

Conal. (He takes Helmet)

The helmet's mine or Leagerie — you are the youngest of us three.

Cuchulain (filling Helmet with ale)

I dont mind which of you keeps it — the Red man gave it for one

But I shall give it to all — to all of us three or to none.

That is as you look upon it — we will pass it to & fro

And him & him always drink out of it & so

[NLI 8761, 16^{r}]

16

singing
Legaire (^with a swaggering stride & gesture)
Legaire is best, [136–151]
Between water & hill
He fought in the west
With cat heads until
At the break of day
All fell by his sword
And he carried away
Their hidden hoard.

Conal.
Give it me – for what did [?you] find in the bag
the the the
But ~~this~~ straw & ~~this~~ broken delf & bits of dirty rag
You d^taken for good money

Cuchullin
No no but give it me
(He takes Helmet)

Conal.
The helmets mine or Legaires – you are the youngest of
us three.

Cuchulan (filling Helmet with ale)
I did not take it to keep it – the Red Man gave it for one
But I shall give it to all – to all of us three or to none –
That is as you look upon it – we will pass it to & fro
And time & time about drink out of it & so

1*sd* singing] singing, *Cuala* stride & gesture] stride *Cuala*
2 water & hill] water and hill, *Cuala*
4 heads until] heads, until *Cuala*
6 sword] sword, *Cuala*
8 hoard.] hoard. (he seizes the Helmet) *Cuala*
9 me – for] me, for *Cuala*
10 straw & the] straw and the *Cuala* delf & the] delf and the *Cuala*
11 You d] You'd *Cuala* money] money? *Cuala*
12 No no but] No, no, but *Cuala* me] me. *Cuala*
13 helmets mine] Helmet's mine *Cuala* Legaires] Leagaire's *Cuala*
14 one] one, *Cuala*
15 none –] none; *Cuala*
16 to & fro] to and fro, *Cuala*
17 time & time about drink] time and time about, drink *Cuala* it & so] it and so *Cuala*

[NLI 8761, 17r]

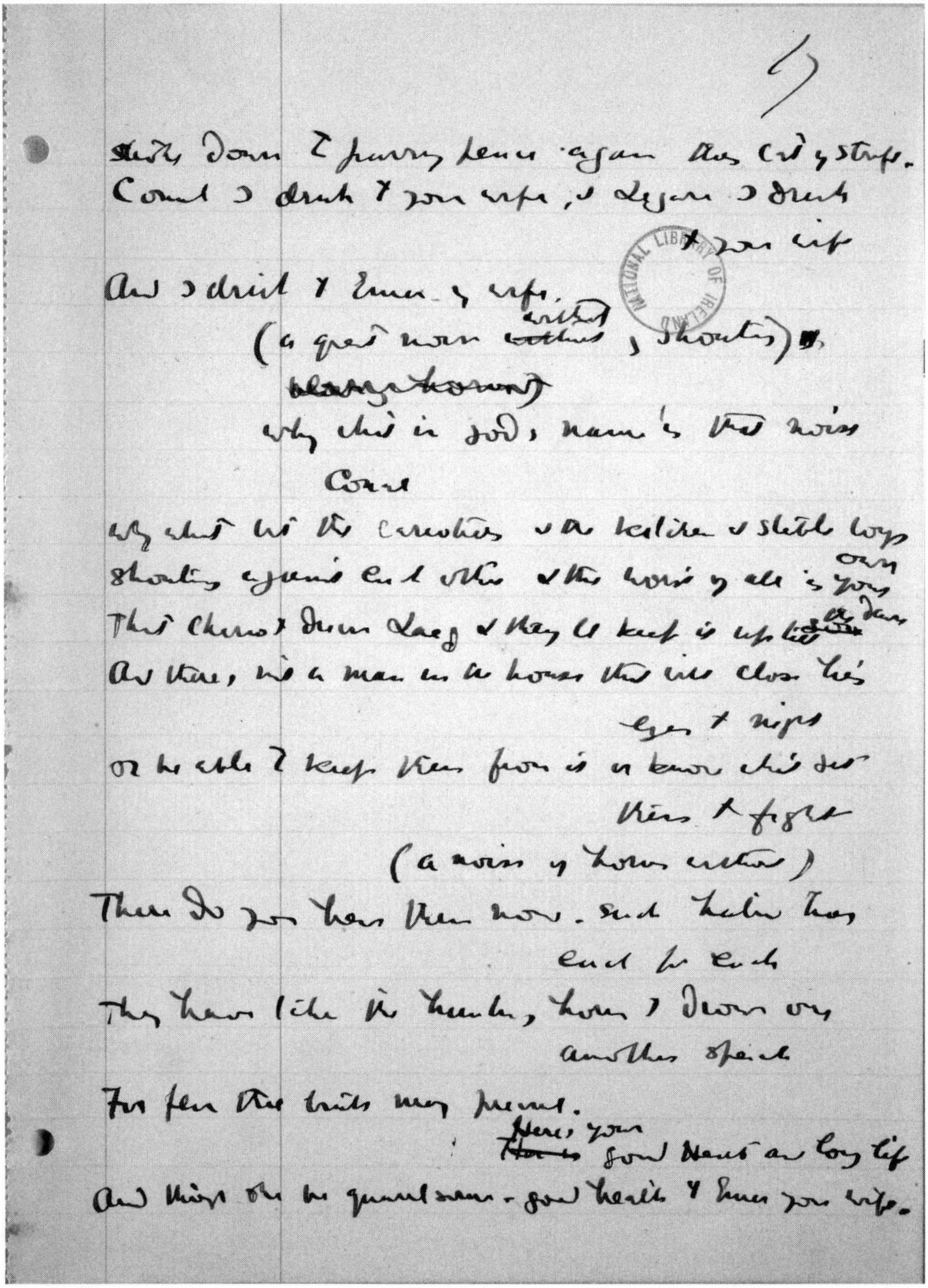

6, 7 Reversing his usual practice, WBY inserted the final words of these lines above rather than below each line.

[NLI 8761, 17[r]]

17

1 Stroke down to purring hence again this cat of strife [152–163]
2 Conal I drink to your wife & Legaire I drink
to your wife
3 And I drink to Emer my wife
without
(a great noise ~~without~~ of shouting ~~&
blaring horns)~~
4 Why what in gods name is that noise

Conal
5 Why what but the carioteers & the kitchen & stable boys
own
6 Shouting against each other & the worst of all is your
the dawn
~~some~~
7 That chariot driver Laeg & they ll keep it up till
8 And theres not a man in the house that will close his
eyes tonight
9 Or be able to keep them from it or know what set
them to fight
(a noise of horns from without)
10 There do you hear them now. Such hatred has
each for each
11 They have take[?n] the hunting horns to drown one
anothers speech
12 For fear the truth may prevail.
Heres your
13 ~~Here is~~ good health and long life
14 And though she be quarrelsome – good health to Emer your wife

---

1 Stroke down to purring hence again this cat of strife] Stroke into peace this cat that has come to take our lives. *Cuala*
2 Conal I drink to your wife & Legaire I drink to your wife] Now it is purring again and now I drink to your wives, *Cuala*
3 Emer my wife] Emer, my wife. *Cuala*
4 why] Why *Cuala* gods name] God's name *Cuala* noise] noise? *Cuala*
5 Why what] What else *Cuala* carioteers & the kitchen stable] Charioteers and the kitchen and stable *Cuala*
6 other & the] other, and the *Cuala*
7 chariot driver Laeg & they ll] chariot-driver, Laeg, and they'll *Cuala* dawn] dawn, *Cuala*
8 theres] there's *Cuala* tonight] to-night, *Cuala*
9 it or] it, or *Cuala* fight] fight. *Cuala*
10 now. Such] now? such *Cuala*
11 anothers] another's *Cuala*
12–13 prevail. / Heres] prevail—here's *Cuala*
14 quarrelsome—good] quarrelsome good *Cuala* Emer your wife] Emer, your wife. *Cuala*

[NLI 8761, 18r]

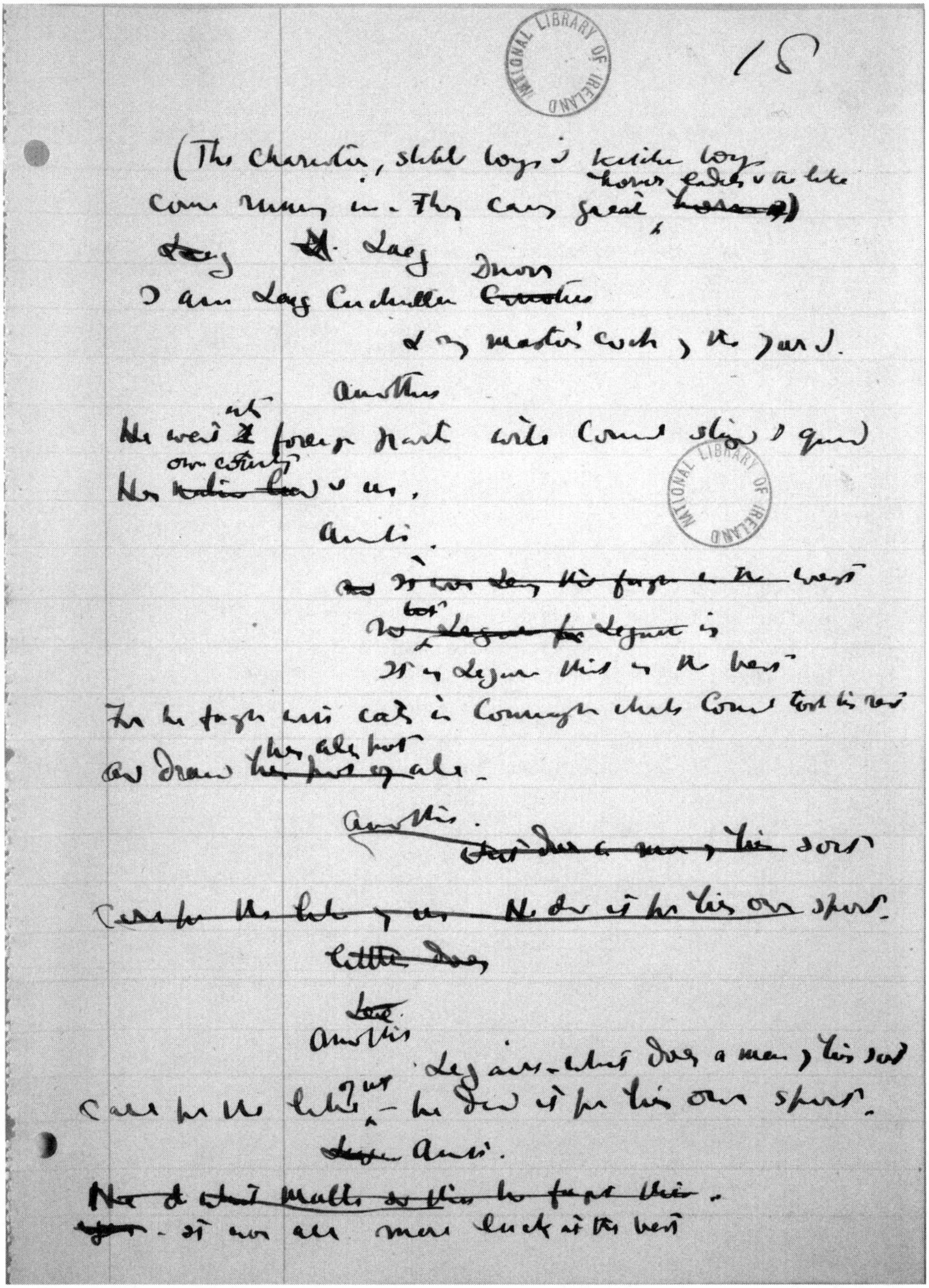
18
NATIONAL LIBRARY OF IRELAND
NATIONAL LIBRARY OF IRELAND

[NLI 8761, 18r]

18

(The charioteer, stable boys, & kitchen boys
horns, ladels & the like
come running in. They carry great^ ~~horns of~~)

~~Laeg~~ ~~L~~ Laeg
Driver
1 I am Laeg Cuchullin ~~Carioteer~~ [164–168]
& my master's cock of the yard.

Another
into
2 He went ~~t~~^ foreign parts wile Conal slept & quit
own country
3 His ~~native land~~ & us.

Anoth.
~~No It was Leary who fought in the west~~
~~but~~
~~No~~^ ~~Legaire for Legaire is~~
4 It is Legaire that is the best
5 For he fought with cats in Connagh while Conal took his rest
his ale pot
6 And draind ~~his pot of ale~~ –

1*sd* charioteer] Charioteers *Cuala* boys, &] boys and *Cuala* ladels & the like] ladles and the like. *Cuala*
1 Laeg Cuchullin Driver &] Laeg, Cuchulain's driver, and *Cuala*
2–3 ANOTHER
Conall would scatter his feathers. (confused murmurs)
LAEGAIRE
(to Cuchulain)
No use, they won't hear a word. *Cuala*
5 Connagh] Connaught *Cuala* Conal] Conall *Cuala*
6 draind] drained *Cuala*

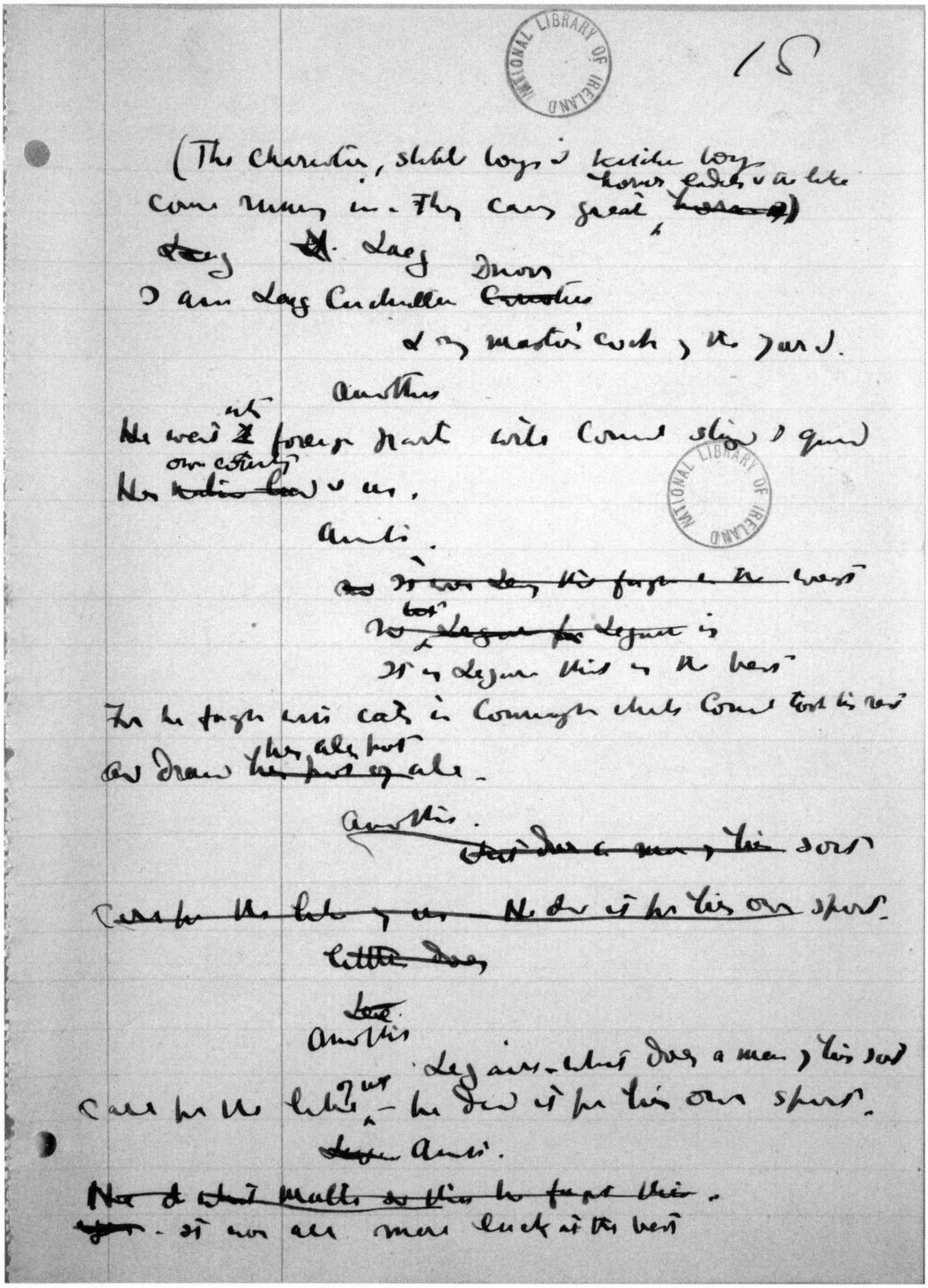
18

(The characters, stable boys & kitchen boys
come running in. They carry great horses, ladles & the like)

Laeg
I am Laeg Cuchullain's Driver
& my master's cock of the yard.

Another
He went at foreign parts while Conal stayed & guarded
His own country & us.

Another.
It is Laegaire this is the best
For he fought with cats in Connaught while Conal took his rest
And drank his ale hot.

Another.
[illegible] sort

Another
Laegaire — what does a man of this sort
Care for the like of us — he does it for his own sport.

Another.
[illegible] — It was all mere luck at the best

[NLI 8761, 18ʳ, continued]

~~Another.~~

~~What does a man of his sort~~

~~Care for the like of us – He did it for his own sport~~ –

~~Cattle driver~~

~~Lae.~~

Another

Legaire – what does a man of his sort [168–170]

of us

Care for the like ^ – he did it for his own sport –

~~Legaire~~ Anoth.

~~He d what mattr so this he forgot this~~ –

~~Yes~~ – It was all mere luck at the best

---

10 like of us – he] like of us? he *Cuala* sport —] sport. *Cuala*

12 best] best. *Cuala*

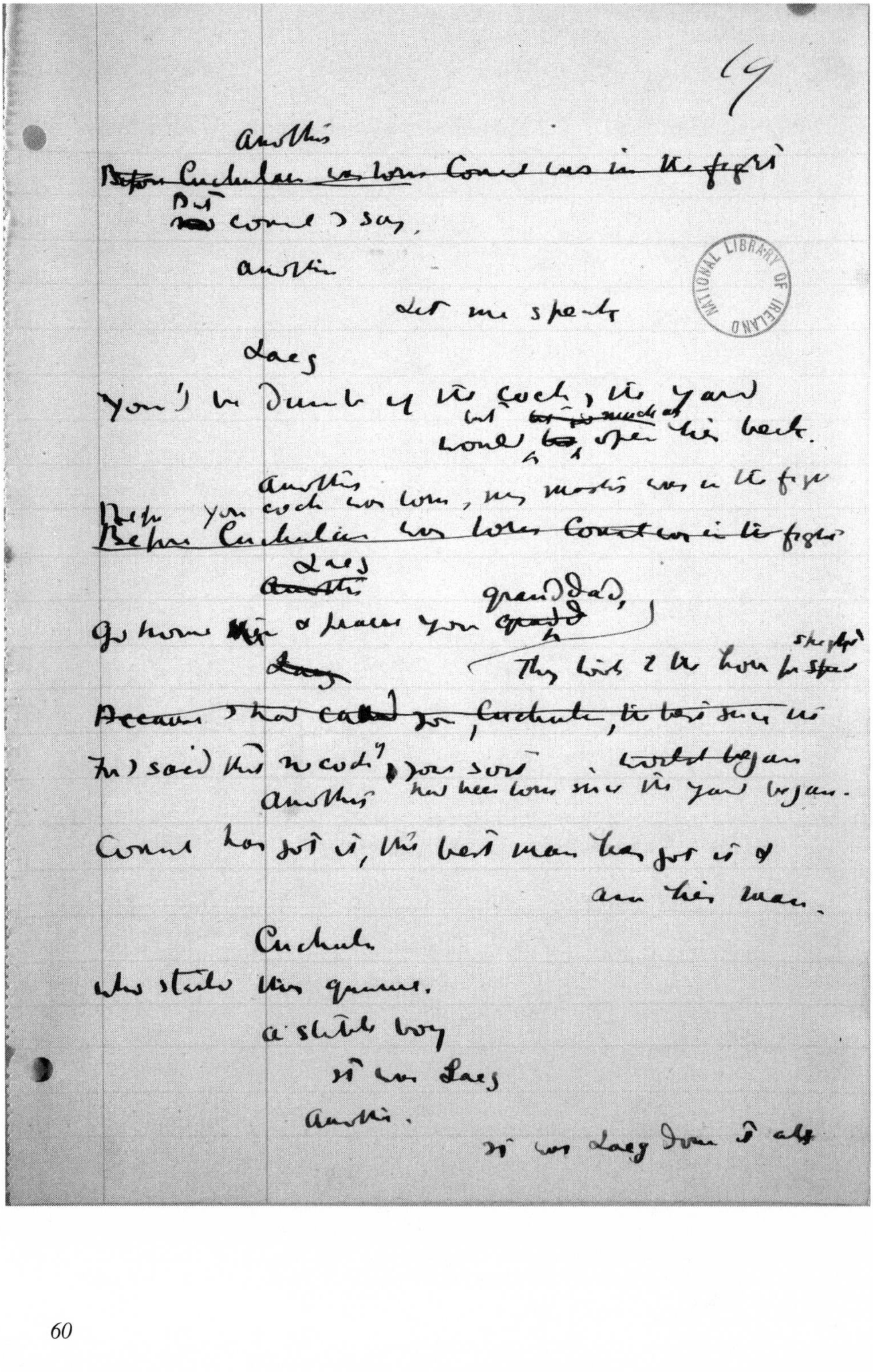

19

Another

~~Before Cuchulain was born Conal was in the fight~~

But
~~[illegible]~~ Conal I say.

Another

Let me speak

Laeg

You'd be dumb if the cock of the yard
would but ~~too~~ so much as open his beak.

Another

~~Before~~ Your cock was born, my master was in the fight

~~Before Cuchulain was born Conal was in the fight~~

Laeg

~~Another~~

Go home ~~[illegible]~~ & please your ~~[illegible]~~ grand dad,

~~Laeg~~ They bid [?] the house for stepfather [?]

~~Because I had called for, Cuchulain, the best since the~~

For I said that no cock of yours ~~world began~~
has been born since the yard began.

Another

Conal has got it, the best man has got it & am his man.

Cuchulain

Who started this quarrel.

A stable boy

It was Laeg

Another.

It was Laeg done it all

[NLI 8761, 19[r]]

19

Another

1 ~~Before Cuchulain was born Conal was in the fight~~

But

2 ~~Now~~ Conal I say. [170–174]

Another

3 Let me speak

Laeg

4 You'd be dumb if the cock of the yard

but ~~but so much as~~

would ^ ~~but~~ ^ open his beak.

Another

Before your cock was born, my master was in the fight

5 ~~Before Cuchulain was born Conal was in the fight~~

Laeg

~~Another~~ granddad,

6 Go home ~~then~~ & praise your ~~grandd~~ ^

~~Laeg~~ spight

7 They took to the horns for ~~spit~~

8 ~~Because I had called you, Cuchulin, the best since the~~

of ~~world began~~

9 For I said that no cock [?~~of~~] your sort

had been born since the yard began.

---

2 Conal I] Conall, I *Cuala*
3 speak] speak. *Cuala*
5 fight] fight. *Cuala*
6 home & praise] home and praise *Cuala* granddad,] grand-dad. *Cuala*
7 spight] spite, *Cuala*
9 yard] fight *Cuala*

19

Another

~~Before Cuchulain was born Conall was in the fight~~

But
~~so~~ Conall I say.

Another

Let me speak

Laeg

You'd be dumb of the cock, the yard
but ~~only so~~ much as
would, ^ ^ open his beak.

Another

~~Before~~ Your cock was born, my master was in the fight
~~Before Cuchulain was born Conall was in the fight~~

Laeg
~~Another~~

grand dad,
Go home ~~[illegible]~~ & praise your ~~grand~~ ^

~~Laeg~~

shepherd
They [?] to the horn [?] for [?]

~~Because I have called you, Cuchulain, the best since the~~

For I said that no cock, your sort ~~world began~~

Another had been born since the yard began.

Conall has got it, the best man has got it & I am his man.

Cuchulain

Who started this quarrel.

A stable boy

It was Laeg

Another.

It was Laeg drew it all [?]

[NLI 8761, 19r, continued]

Another

10 Conal has got it, the best man has got it &
am his man. [175–176]

Cuchuln

11 Who started this quarrel.

A stable boy

12 It was Laeg

Another.

13 It was Laeg done it all

---

10 Conal] Conall *Cuala* got it &] got it, and I *Cuala* man] man. *Cuala*
11 quarrel.] quarrel? *Cuala*
12 Laeg] Laeg. *Cuala*
13 all] all. *Cuala*

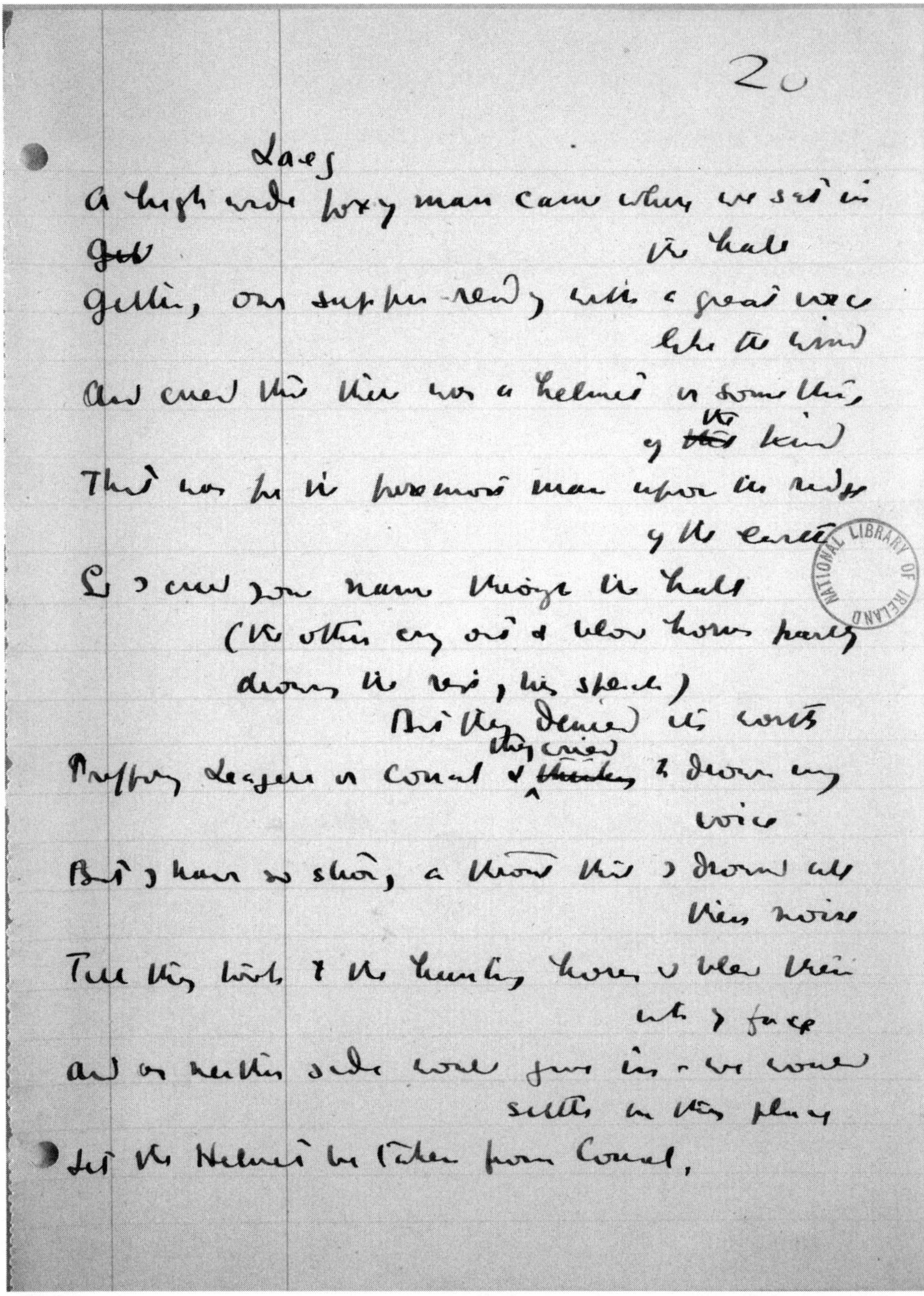

20

Laeg

A high wide foxy man came where we sat in
~~got~~ the hall
getting our supper ready with a great voice
like the wind
And cried that there was a helmet or something
of ~~that~~ the kind
That was for the foremost man upon the ridge
of the earth
Laeg I cried your name through the hall
(the others cry out & blow horns partly
drowning the rest, his speech)
But they denied its worth
Proffering Leagere or Conal & ~~thinking~~ they cried to drown my
voice
But I have so strong a throat that I drowned all
their noise
Till they took to the hunting horns & blew them
into my face
And as neither side would give in — we would
settle in this place
Let the Helmet be taken from Conal,

[NLI 8761, 20r]

20

Laeg

1 A high wide foxy man came where we sat in
the hall [177–186]

~~Get~~

2 Getting our supper ready with a great voice
like the wind

3 And cried that there was a helmet or something
the
of ~~this~~ kind

4 That was fo th fore most man upon the ridge
of the earth

5 So I cried your name through the hall

(the others cry out and blow horns partly
drowning the rest of his speech)

6 But they denied its worth
they cried

7 Preferring Leagarie or Conal & ^ ~~thinking~~ to drown my
voice

8 But I have so strong a throat that I drownd all
their noise

9 Till they took to the hunting horns & blew them
into my face

10 And as neither side would give in – we would
settle in this place

11 Let the Helmet be taken from Conal.

---

1 hall] hall, *Cuala*
2 ready with] ready, with *Cuala* wind] wind, *Cuala*
4 fo th fore most] for the foremost *Cuala* earth] earth. *Cuala*
7 Leagarie or Conal &] Laegaire or Conall and *Cuala* voice] voice; *Cuala*
8 drownd] drowned *Cuala*
9 horns & blew] horns and blew *Cuala* face] face, *Cuala*
10 place] place. *Cuala*
11 Conal] Conall *Cuala*

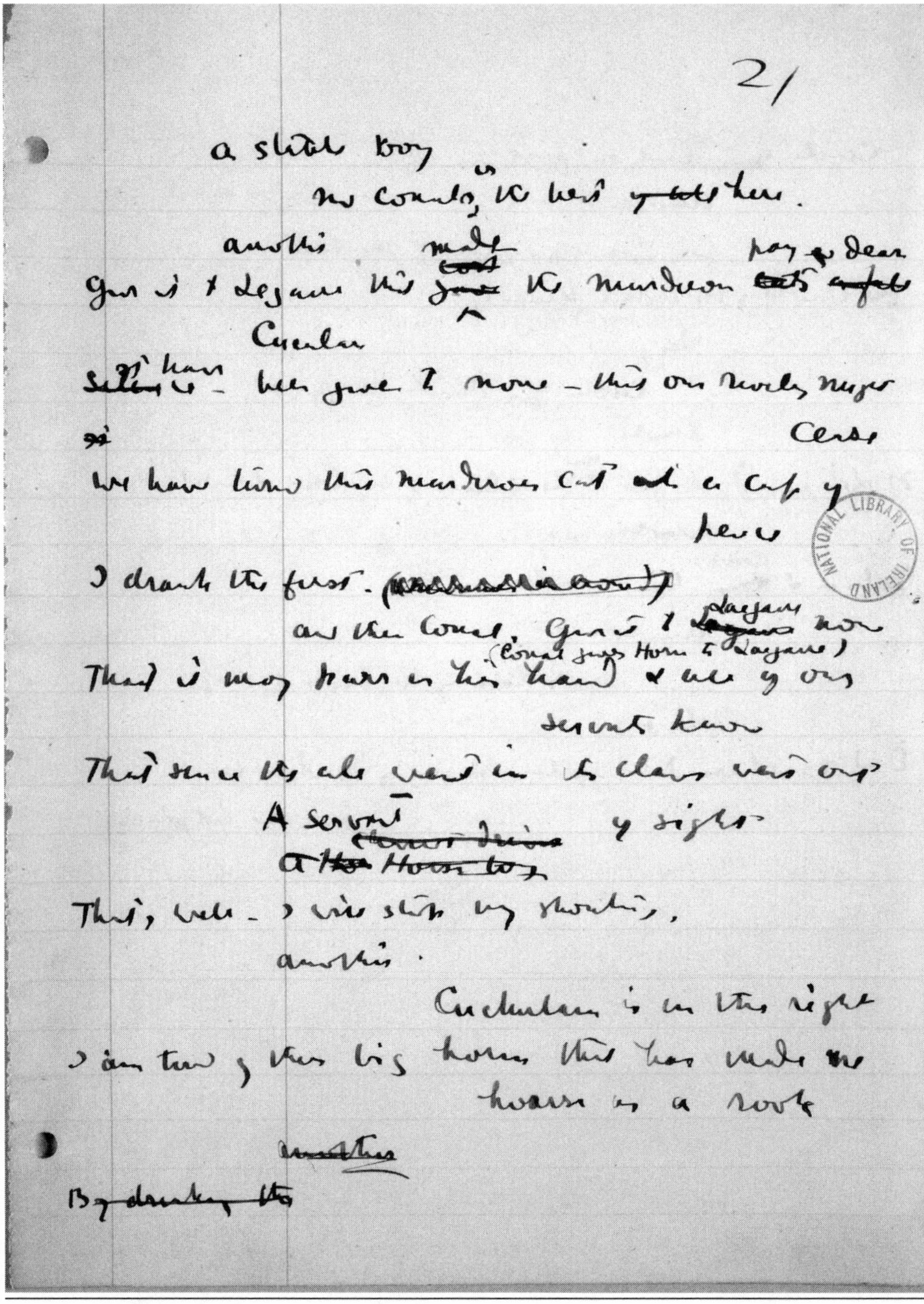

21

a second boy

No Conals, the best is of all here.

another — made

Give it to Legaire that ~~cost~~ the murderous ~~cats~~ pay dear

Cuchulain

~~Settled~~ It has — been given to none — this our nightly wager

cease

We have turned this murderous cat into a cup of peace

I drank the first. ~~(~~~~~~)~~

and then Conal, Give it to Laegaire now (Conal gives Horn to Laegaire)

That it may pass in his hand & all of our servants know

That since the ale went in the claws went out of sight

A servant ~~Horse dealer~~ ~~A Horn boy~~

That, well — I will stop my shouting,

another.

Cuchulain is in the right

I am tired of this big horn that has made me hoarse as a rook

~~another~~

~~By drinking the~~

1 No Conals] No, Conall *Cuala* best here] best man here *Cuala*
2 murderous pay dear] murderous cats pay dear. *Cuala*
3 cease] cease, *Cuala*
4 peace] peace, *Cuala*

[NLI 8761, 21r]

21

A stable boy
is
1 No Conals ^ the best ~~of all~~ here. [186–194]

Another
made
~~cost~~ pay [?~~so~~/~~as~~] dear
2 Give it to Legaire that ~~gave~~ ^ the murderous ~~cats~~ ~~in full~~

Cuculan
It has
3 ~~Silence~~ – been given to none – that our rivalry might
cease
~~It~~
4 We have turned that murderous cat into a cup of
peace
5 I drank the first – (~~murmers in crowd~~)
Laegaire
6 and then Conal. Give it to ~~Legaire~~ now
(Conal gives Horn to Laegaire)
7 That it may purr in his hand & all of our
servants know
8 That since the ale went in its claws went out
of sight

A servant
~~Chariot driver~~
~~A Hor Horse boy~~
9 That s well – I will stop my shouting.

Another.
10 Cuchulain is in the right
11 I am tired of this big horn that has made me
hoarse as a rook

~~Another~~
~~By drinking the~~

5–6 I drank the first. / And then Conal. Give it] I drank the first; and then Conall; give it *Cuala*
6*sd* Horn] horn *Cuala*
7 hand & all] hand and all *Cuala*
8 sight] sight. *Cuala*
9 That s] That's *Cuala*
10 right] right; *Cuala*
11 rook] rook. *Cuala*

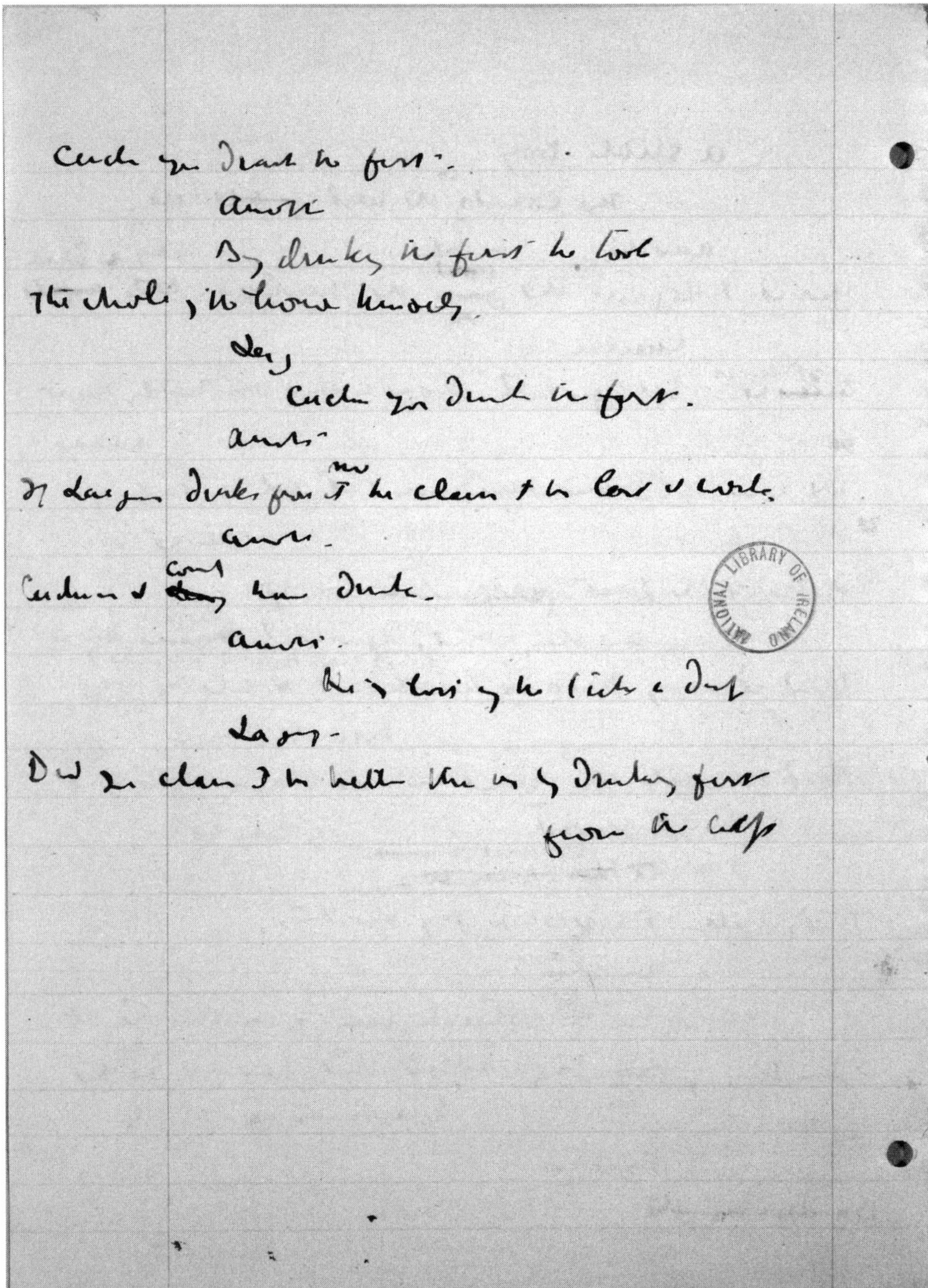
NATIONAL LIBRARY OF IRELAND

[NLI 8761, 21ᵛ]

Cuch you drank the first. [196–199]

Anothr

By drinking the first he took
the whole of the honour himself.

Leag

Cuchu you drank the first

Anothr –

now
If Laegaire drinks from it he claims to be last & worst

Anoth.

Conal
Cuchulain & ~~Leag~~ have drunk.

Anoth.

He is lost if he licks a drop

Lagr –

Did you claim to be better than us by drinking first
from the cup

1–4, 8 These lines repeat what is found on the facing page, 22ʳ.

5–7 Replacement lines for ll. 5–7 on 22ʳ. They correspond to the reading in *Cuala* but with some verbal differences (see the *apparatus criticus* on p. 71).

[NLI 8761, 22r]

22

Laeg

Cuchulain you drank the first

Another

By drinking the first he took
The whole of the honour himself & left our
master naught.

Laeg (~~laying~~ ha

Cuchulain you drank the first

Another

Leagaire is all he
~~is all day when~~ he thought

~~of Leagaire drink first it now he admits~~
~~himself for the worst~~

If you drink out of it now you admit yourself
the worst

Leagaire (laying horn on table)

Did you claim to be better than you
Cuchulain by drinking first?

Cuchulain (His words are
partly drowned by the murmurs of the crowd
though he speaks very loud)

That juggler from the sea that old Red
Herring it is
who has set us all by the ears. He brought the
Helmet for this.

[NLI 8761, 22r]

22

Laeg

1 Cuchulain you drank the first [196–201]

Another

2 By drinking the first he took

3 The whole of the honour himself & left our masters naught.

Laeg (~~laying ho~~

4 Cuchulain you drank the first

Another

5 Legaire it will be ~~It will evry where be~~ thought

6 ~~If Legaire drinks from it now he admits himself for the worst~~

7 If you drink out of it now you admit yourself the worst

Legaire (laying horn on table)

8 Did you claim to be better than you Cuchulan by drinking first?

Cuchulan (His words are partly drowned by the murmurs of the crowd) though he speaks very loud)

9 That juggler from the sea that old Red Herring it is

10 Who has set us all by the ears. —he brought the Helmet for this.

---

1 Cuchulain you] Cuchulain, you *Cuala* first] first. *Cuala*

3 honour himself] honours himself. *Cuala* & left our masters naught. *lacking in Cuala*

4 Cuchulain you] Cuchulain, you *Cuala* first] first. *Cuala*

5–7 ANOTHER

If Laegaire drink from it now he claims to be last and worst.

ANOTHER

Cuchulain and Conall have drunk.

ANOTHER

He is lost if he taste a drop. *Cuala*

8 Did you claim to better than us by drinking first from the cup? *Cuala*

9 sea that] sea, that *Cuala* Red Herring] red herring *Cuala*

10 this.] this, *Cuala*

4*sd* WBY began and then aborted the word "horn" here. See the stage direction above l. 8 on 22r.

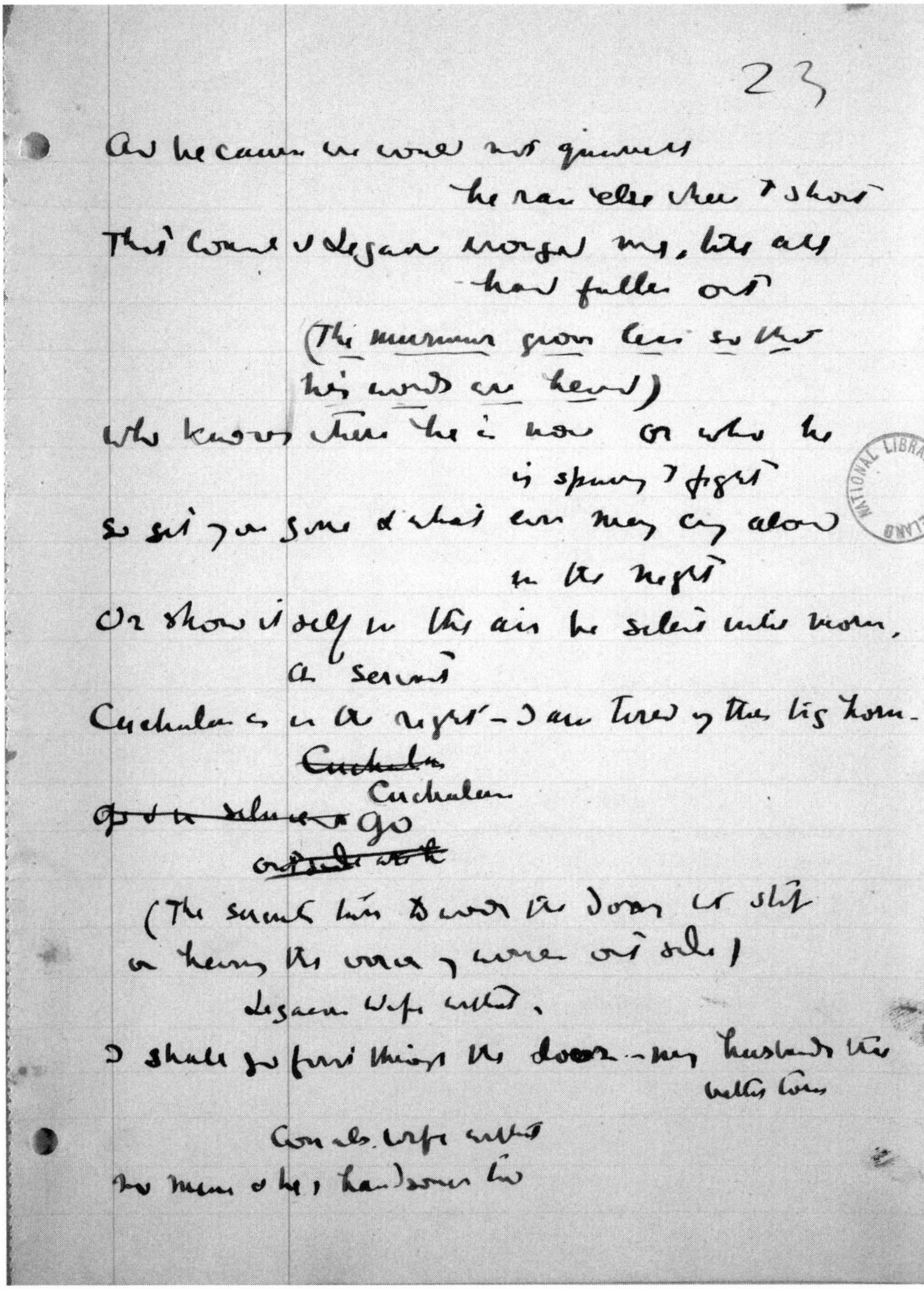
And because we would not quarrel
he ran there to shout
That Conal & Legaire brought me, have all
have fallen out
(The murmur grows less so that
his words are heard)
Who knows where he is now or who he
is sparring to fight
So set your song of what men may cry aloud
in the night
Or show itself in the air be silent until morning.
A servant
Cuchulain is in the night — I am tired of this big horn.
~~Cuchulain~~
Cuchulain
~~Go & be silent~~ go
~~outside work~~
(The servant turns towards the door or stops
on hearing the voices of women outside.)
Legaire's Wife without.
I shall go first through the door — my husband the
better born
Conal's Wife without
No man of his handsomer ...

[NLI 8761, 23r]

23

1 And because we would not quarrell [202–208]
he ran else where to shout
2 That Conal & Legaire wronged me, till all
had fallen out

(The murmur grows less so that
his words are heard)

3 Who knows where he is now or who he
is spurring to fight
4 So get you gone & what ever may cry aloud
in the night
5 Or show itself in the air be silent until morn.

A servant
6 Cuchulain is in the right – I am tired of this big horn.

~~Cuchulan~~
Cuchulan
7 ~~Go & in silence~~ Go
~~outside with~~

(The servants turn towards the door but stop
on hearing the voices of women outside)

Legaires Wife without.
8 I shall go first through the door – my husbands the
better born

Conals wife without
9 No Mine & hes handsomer too

---

1 quarrell] quarrel *Cuala* else where] elsewhere *Cuala*
2 Conal & Legaire] Conall and Laegaire *Cuala* out] out. *Cuala*
2*sd* The] the *Cuala* *no italics in Cuala*
3 fight] fight? *Cuala*
4 gone & what ever] gone, and whatever *Cuala* night] night, *Cuala*
5 air be] air, be *Cuala*
7 Go] Go. *Cuala*
7*sd* The] the *Cuala*
8–9 LAEGAIRE'S WIFE
(without) Mine is the better to look at.
CONALL'S WIFE
(without) But mine is better born. *Cuala*

8, 9 sd without] That is, speaking from off stage.

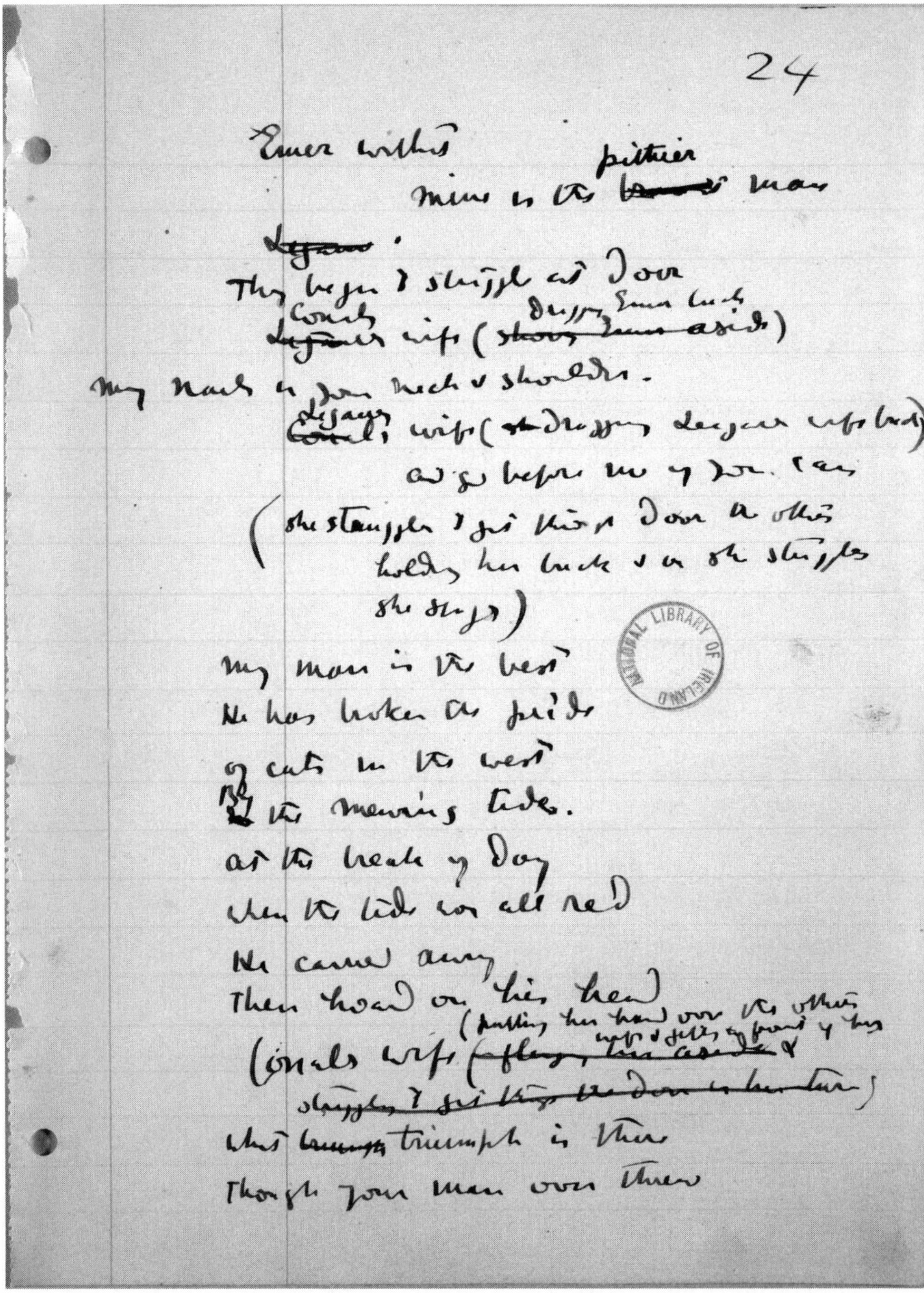
24

Emer writhes

mine is the ~~bravest~~ pithier man

~~Laegaire~~

They begin to struggle at door

~~Laegaires~~ Conals wife (~~shoves Emer aside~~ dragging Emer back)

My nails in your neck & shoulders.

~~Conals~~ Laegaires wife (~~st~~ dragging Laegaire wife back)

and go before me if you can

(she struggles to get through door the other holding her back & as she struggles she sings)

My man is the best

He has broken the pride

Of cats in the west

By the mewing tide.

At the break of day

When the tide was all red

He carried away

Their hoard on his head

(Conals wife (~~flinging her aside~~ putting her hand over the others mouth & getting in front of her & struggles to get through the door in her turn)

What ~~triumph~~ triumph is there

Though your man overthrew

[NLI 8761, 24r]

24

Emer without

pithier

1 Mine is the ~~bravest~~ man [209–214]

~~Legaire~~.

They begin to struggle at door

Conals dragging Emer back

~~Legaires~~ wife (~~shovng Emer aside~~)

2 My nails in your neck & shoulder.

Legaires

~~Conals~~ wife (~~sh~~ dragging Legaires wife back)

3 And go before me if you can

(she struggles to get through door the others
holding her back & as she struggles
she sings)

---

1 Mine] My man *Cuala* man] man. *Cuala*

1*sd* (The women come to the door struggling) *Cuala*

1/2 CUCHULAIN

Old hurricane, well done

You've set our wives to the game that they may egg us on;
We are to kill each other that you may sport with us.
Ah, now, they've begun to wrestle as to who'll be first at the house.
(The women come to the door struggling)

EMER

No, I have the right of place for I married the better man. *Cuala*

2*sd* dragging Emer] pulling Emer *Cuala* (she struggles to . . . others / holding . . . struggles / she sings) *lacking Cuala*

2 neck & shoulder] neck and shoulder. *Cuala*

3*sd* Legaires] Legaire's *Cuala*

3 can] can. *Cuala*

1*sd* WBY entered the part ascription for Laegaire, canceled it, and then added the stage direction, omitting the usual parentheses. Before publication he expanded the passage to include Cuchulain's response to the Red Man.

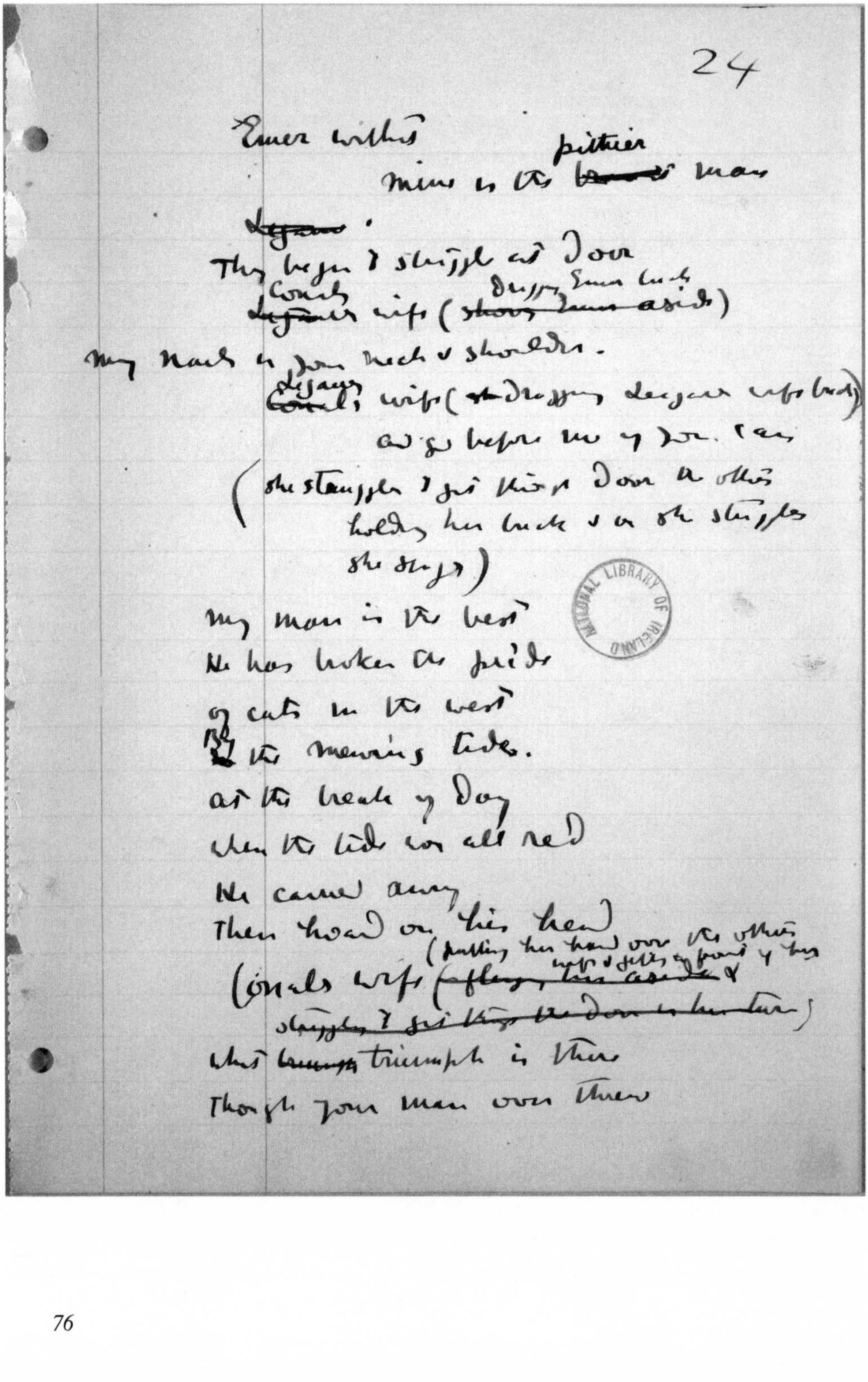

24

Emer within

pitier
mine is the ~~braver~~ man

~~Loegaire~~.

They begin to struggle at door

Conals dragging Emer back
~~Loegaires~~ wife (~~shoves Emer aside~~)

My hand is on your neck & shoulders.

Loegaires
~~Conals~~ wife (~~st~~ dragging Loegaires wife back)

and go before me if you can

(She struggles to get through door the other
holding her back & as she struggles
she sings)

My man is the best
He has broken the pride
Of cats in the west
By the moving tide.
At the break of day
When the tide was all red
He carried away
Their hoard on his head

(putting her hand over the others
mouth & getting in front of her
Conals wife (~~flinging her aside~~ &
~~struggles to get through the door in her turn~~)

What ~~triumph~~ triumph is there
Though your man over there

[NLI 8761, 24ʳ, continued]

My man is the best [215]
He has broken the pride
Of cats in the west
By
~~In~~ the mewing tide.
At the break of day
When the tide was all red
He carried away
Their hoard on his head
(putting her hand over the others
naps & getting in front of them
Conals Wife ~~(flinging her aside~~ &
~~struggles to get through the door in her turn~~)
What ~~triumph~~ triumph is there
Though your man over there

5–14 My husband fought in the West.
CONALL'S WIFE
(kneeling in the door so as to keep the others out who pull at her)
But what did he fight with there
But sidelong and spitting and helpless shadows of the dim air?
And what did he carry away but straw and broken delf?
LAEGAIRE'S WIFE
Your own man made up that tale trembling alone by himself
Drowning his terror. *Cuala*

12sd WBY wrote "naps" for "napes" (that is, Emer holds the two women back by their necks and pushes through to the front).

[NLI 8761, 25r]

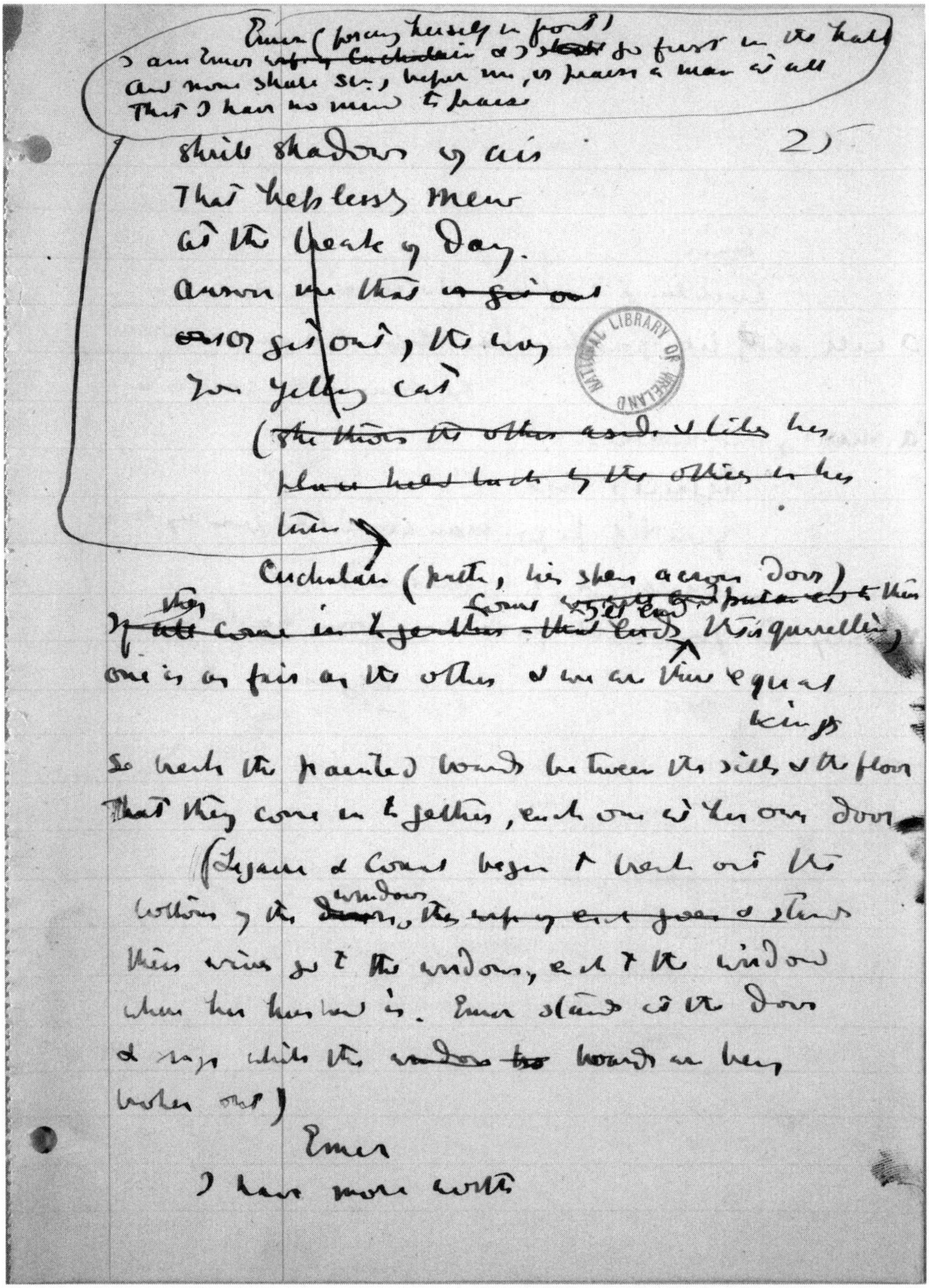
Emer (forcing herself in front)
I am Emer wife of Cuchulain & I ~~shall~~ go first in the hall
And none shall sing before me, or praise a man at all
That I have no need to praise

25

Shrill shadows of air
That helplessly mew
At the break of day.
Answer me that is ~~going out~~
~~or~~ or get out, the way
Your yelling cat
(~~She throws the other aside & takes her place holds back the other~~ in her turn)

Cuchulain (putting his spear across door)
~~If all come in together – that lords~~ ... the quarrelling
one is as fair as the other & we are three equal kings
So break the painted boards between the sills & the floor
That they come in together, each one at her own door
(Laegaire & Conal begin to break out the bottoms of the ~~doors~~ windows, their ~~wife of each goes & stands~~ wives go to the windows, each to the window where her husband is. Emer stands at the door & says while the ~~windows~~ ~~too~~ boards are being broken out)

Emer
I have more worth

[NLI 8761, 25^{r}]

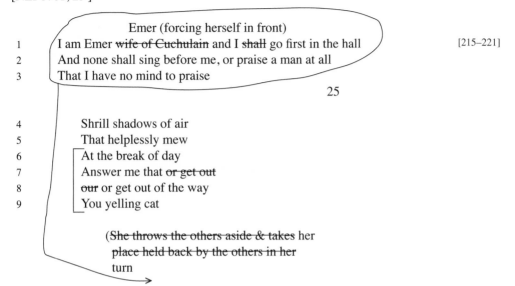

Emer (forcing herself in front)
I am Emer ~~wife of Cuchulain~~ and I ~~shall~~ go first in the hall [215–221]
And none shall sing before me, or praise a man at all
That I have no mind to praise

25

Shrill shadows of air
That helplessly mew
At the break of day
Answer me that ~~or get out~~
~~our~~ or get out of the way
You yelling cat

(~~She throws the others aside & takes~~ her
~~place held back by the others in her~~
turn

---

1 Emer and I go first in the hall] Emer, it is I go first through the door. *Cuala*
2 And none shall sing] No one shall walk *Cuala* a man at all] any man before *Cuala*
3 That I have no mind to praise] My man has been praised *Cuala*
4–9, 9*sd* *lacking in Cuala*

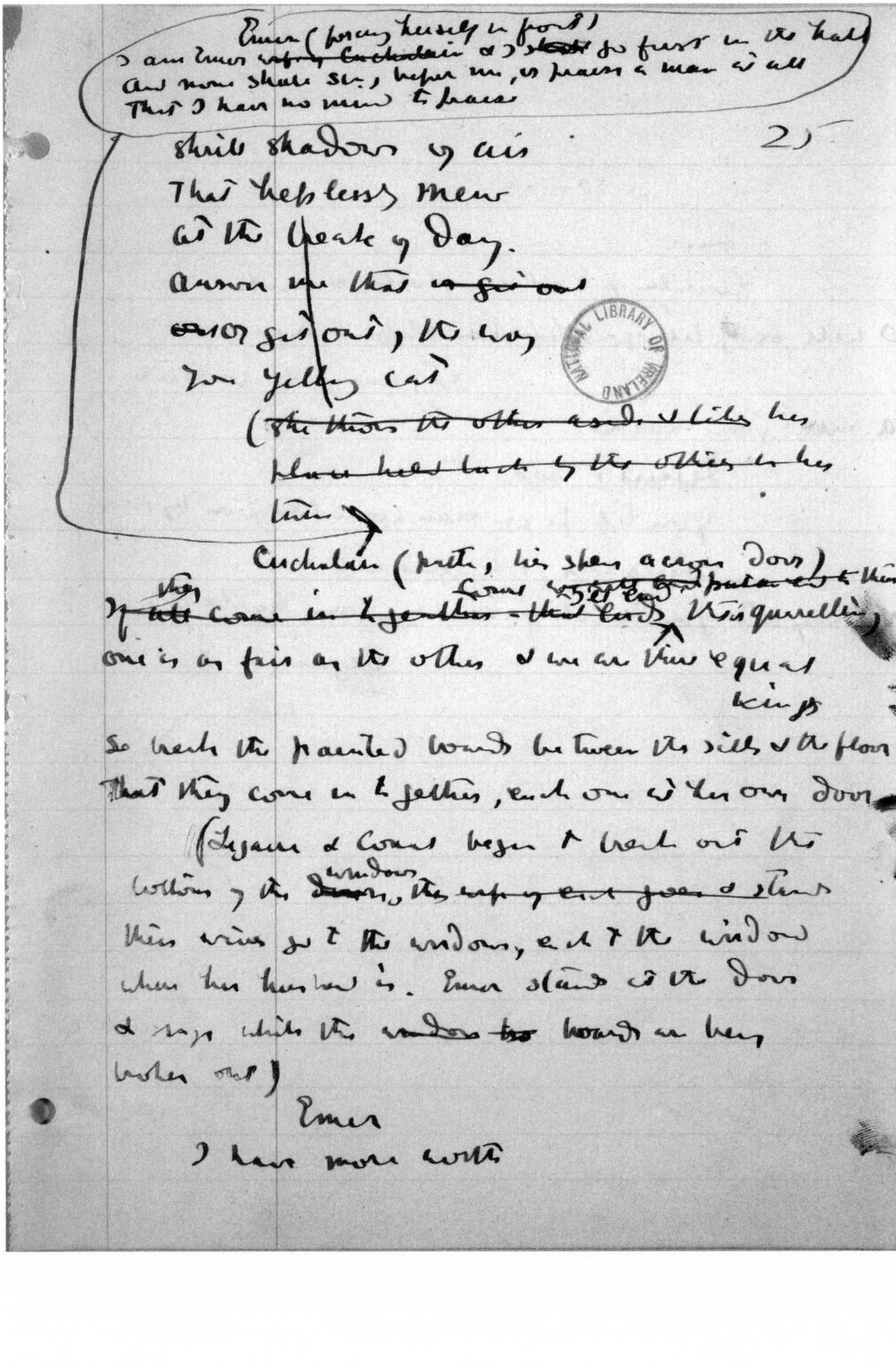
Emer (forcing herself in front)
I am Emer ~~wife of Cuchulain~~ & I ~~shall~~ go first in the hall
And none shall sit, before me, or pass a man at all
That I have no mind to pass

shrill shadows of air
That hapless mew
At the break of day.
Answer me that ~~is going out~~
~~or~~ or go out, the way
Some yelling cat
(~~She throws the other aside & takes her~~
~~place hold back by the other in her~~
~~turn~~)

Cuchulain (putting his spear across door)
~~If they come in together — that lord~~ Its quarrelling
one is as fair as the other & we are three equal kings
So break the painted boards between the sill & the floor
That they come in together, each one at her own door

(Laegaire & Conal begin to break out the
bottoms of the ~~doors~~ windows, they ~~wife of each goes & stand~~
their wives go to the windows, each to the window
where her husband is. Emer stands at the door
& says while the ~~window two~~ boards are being
broken out)

Emer
I have more worth

25

[NLI 8761, 25[r], continued]

Cuchulan (putting his spear across door)

~~we shall end~~ ~~put an end to their~~

~~they~~ Come I'll end ir}

~~If all come in together – that ends~~^ the }quarrelling [221–224]

One is as fair as the other & we are three equal kings

So break the painted boards between the sills & the floor

That they come in together, each one at her own door –

(Legaire & Conal begin to break out the windows

bottoms of the ~~doors~~, ~~the wife of each goes & stands~~ Their wives go to the windows, each to the window where her husband is. Emer stands at the door & sings while the ~~windows~~ ~~bro~~ boards are being broken out)

Emer

I have more worth

---

10 (putting his spear across door)] (spreading his arms across the door so as to close it) *Cuala* Come I'll end this] Come, put an end to their *Cuala*

11 other & we are three equal kings] other and each one the wife of a king. *Cuala*

12 So break] Break down *Cuala* sills & the floor] sill and the floor *Cuala*

13 door –] door. *Cuala*

13*sd* windows / Their] windows, then their *Cuala* & sings] and sings *Cuala* broken out)] broken out.) *Cuala*

14 *lacking in Cuala*

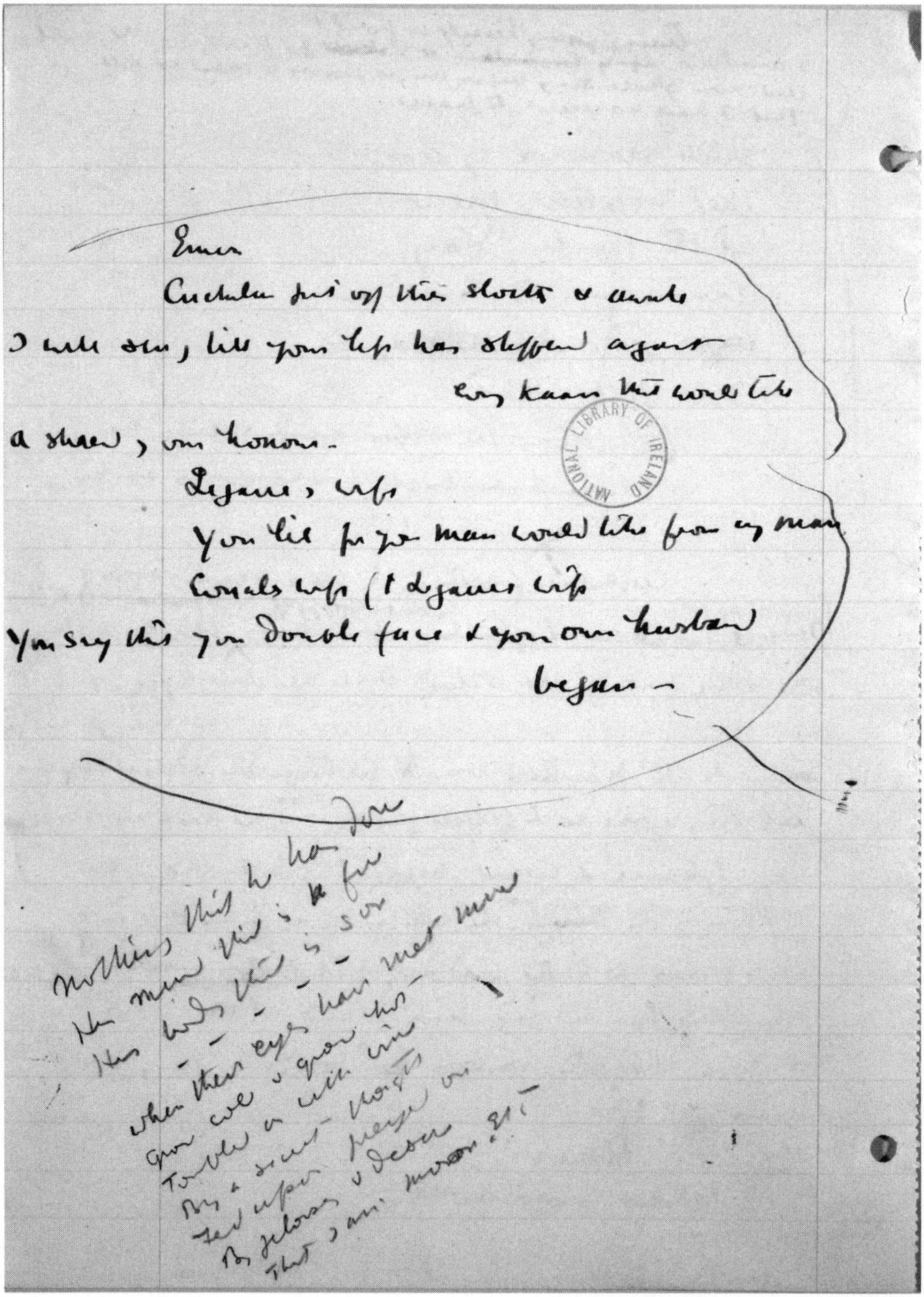

Emer
Cuchulain dies of this slander & insult
I will see, till your lips has stiffened again
Every knave that would take
a share of our honour.
Eithne's lips
You lie for your man would take from any man
Conall's wife (of Eithne's lips
You say this your double face & your own husband
began—

Nothing that he has done
His mind that is the fire
His body that is the sod
— — —
When their eyes have met mine
Grow cold & grow hot
Troubled or with anger
By a secret thought
Fed upon jealousy & desire
That I am mirror etc

[NLI 8761, 25[v]]

Emer

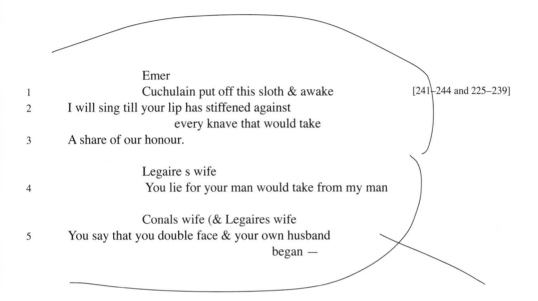

1 Cuchulain put off this sloth & awake [241–244 and 225–239]

2 I will sing till your lip has stiffened against
every knave that would take

3 A share of our honour.

Legaire s wife

4 You lie for your man would take from my man

Conals wife (& Legaires wife

5 You say that you double face & your own husband
began —

6 *Nothing that he has done*
7 *His mind that is a fire*
8 *His body that is sun*
- - - - -
9 *When their eyes have met mine*
10 *Grow cold & grow hot*
11 *Troubled as with wine*
12 *By a secret thought*
13 *Fed upon preyed on*
14 *By jealousy & desire*
15 *That I am moon, Etc*

1–5 Revision of the first six lines on 27[r] and marked for insertion at l. 16 on 26[r].

6–8 The lines in pencil revise ll. 16–18 on 26[r].

9–10 These lines revise ll. 24–30 on 26[r]. The *Cuala* text shows further revision of the entire song (see the *apparatus criticus* on p. 85).

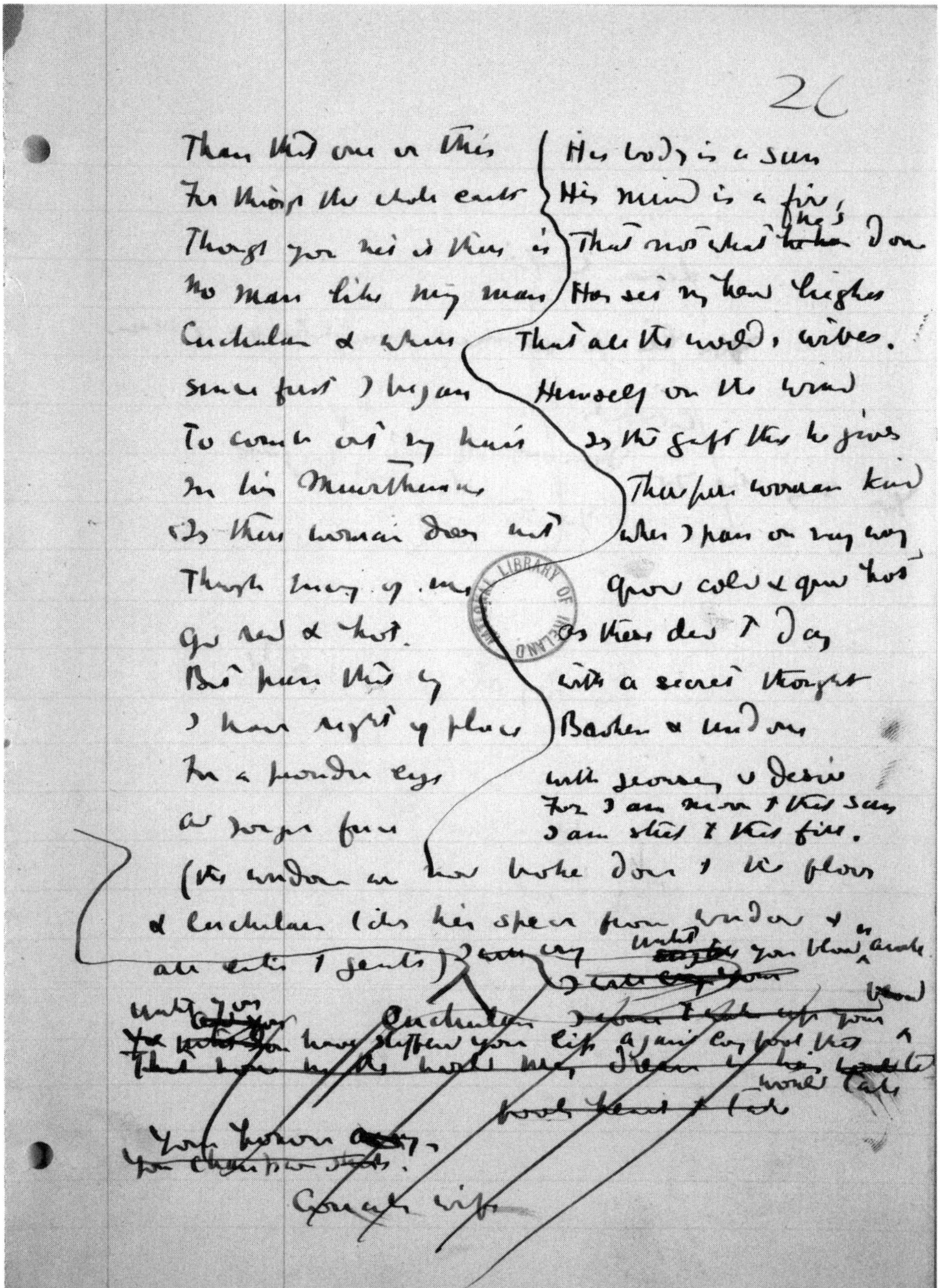
Than that one or this
For things the whole earth
Though you see it there is
No man like my man
Cuchulain & where
since first I began
To comb out my hair
In his Muirthemne
As there woman does not
Though many of my
grow red & hot.
But pass that by
I have right of place
For a prouder eye
Or longer fame

His body is a sun
His mind is a fire,
That not what he's done
Has set my heart higher
That all the world's wives.
Herself on the wind
As the gift there to give
That few women kind
when I pass on my way
Grow cold & grow hot
As there dew & day
with a secret thought
Broken & undone
with jealousy & desire
For I am moon to that sun
I am steel to that fire.

(the window are now broke down to the floors
& Cuchulain lets his spear from window & is
all eyes & gentle)

Cuchulain

Your honour

Conall's wife

[NLI 8761, 26^{r}]

26

[225–240]

Then that one or this
For through the whole earth
Though you [?nil] it there is
No man like my man
Cuchulan & where
Since first I began
To comb out my hair
In his Muirthemne
Is there woman does not
Through envy of me
Go red & hot.
But pass that by
I have right of place
For a prouder eye
And younger face

His body is a sun
His mind is a fire,
he's
That not what ~~he has~~ done
Has set my head higher
That all the worlds wives.
Himself on the wind
Is the gift that he gives
Therefore woman kind
When I pass on my way
Grow cold & grow hot
As these did t day
With a secret thought
Broken & undone
With jealousy & desire
For I am moon to that sun
I am steel to that fire.

1–31 Nothing that he has done,
His mind that is fire,
His body that is sun,
Have set my head higher,
Than all the world's wives.
Himself on the wind
Is the gift that he gives,
Therefore women kind,
When their eyes have met mine,
Grow cold and grow hot
Troubled as with wine
By a secret thought,
Preyed upon, fed upon
By jealousy and desire,
For I am moon to that sun,
I am steel to that fire. *Cuala*

WBY may have intended the right hand column to replace the left hand column of Emer's song, but he did not cancel either column, even after entering the pencil revision of ll. 16–18 and 24–30 on 25^{v}. This ink version on 26^{r}, perhaps including the revisions on 25^{v}, was probably meant to consist of all thirty-one lines and was later shortened to sixteen lines when the next iteration, either a fair copy or a typescript that is now missing, was prepared.

3 WBY may be using the queried word "nil" in the archaic sense "not to will, to refuse," or in other words, to deny (*OED*).

26 For "t day" read "today."

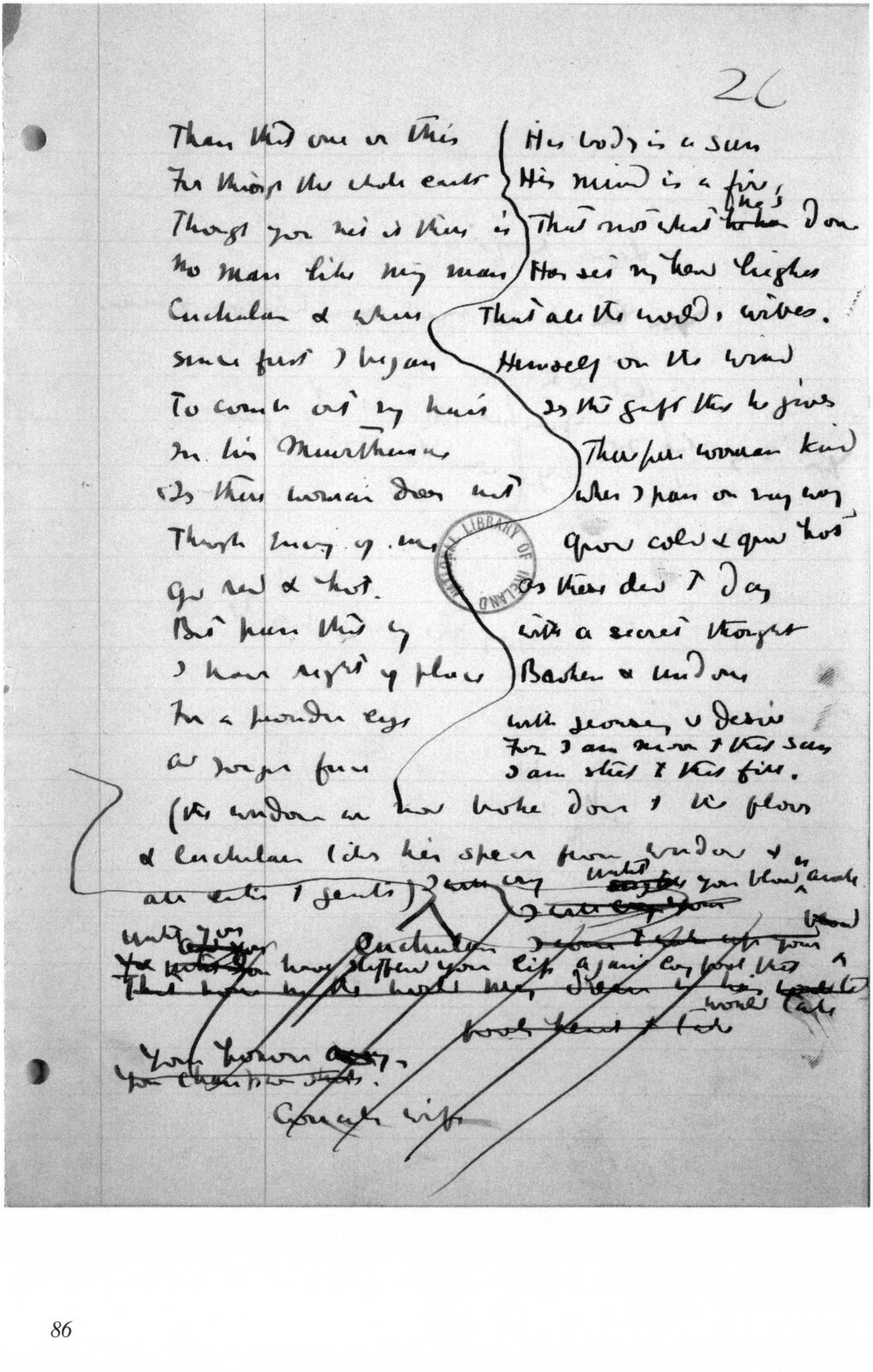
26

Than that one or this
For though the whole earth
Though you seek it there is
No man like my man
Cuchulain & when
since first I began
To comb out my hair
In his Muirthemne
As there woman does not
Though envy of me
Go red & hot.
But pass that by
I have right of place
In a prouder eye
As yonder face

His body is a sun
His mind is a fire,
That not what he's I own
Has set my head higher
That all the world's wives.
Herself on the wind
As the gift that he gives
Therefore woman kind
When I pass on my way
Grow cold & grow hot
As these dew & day
With a secret thought
Broken & undone
With jealousy & desire
For I am moon to that sun
I am steel to that fire.

(the window on her broke down & the floor
& Cuchulain lifts his spear from window & all enter & gentle)

Cuchulain

Your honours

[NLI 8761, 26[r], continued]

(the windows are now broke down to the floor
& Cuchulan takes his spear from window &
all enter to gents)^

me
I will cry until you blow ^ aside [241–243]
~~sing till~~
I will ~~cry~~ your ~~blood~~
32 Cuchulan ~~I come to wake up your~~ ^
Until you
~~And you~~
~~Yo~~ ~~Until you~~ have stiffened your lip against every fool that
33 ~~That [?knaves] in the world may dream in his~~ ~~would~~
~~would take~~
~~fools heart & take~~
Your honour ~~away~~ –
34 ~~Your champion ship~~.

Conals wife

32*sd* (The windows are now broken down to floor. Cuchulain takes his spear from the door, and the three women come in at the same moment) *Cuala*

32 EMER
Cuchulain, put off this sloth and awake,
I will sing till I've stiffened your lip against every knave that would take
A share of our honour. *Cuala*

---

32 The misprint in *Cuala*, "our honour," was corrected to "your honour" in *The Green Helmet and Other Poems* (New York: Macmillan, 1911; Wade 85).

32–34 These lines, a continuation of Emer's appeal to Cuchulain, are heavily revised here before cancellation, reworked on 27[r] and canceled, and finally revised on 25[v], where they are marked with an arrow for insertion at the end of the *sd* above l. 32 on 26[r] (shown above)

[NLI 8761, 26v]

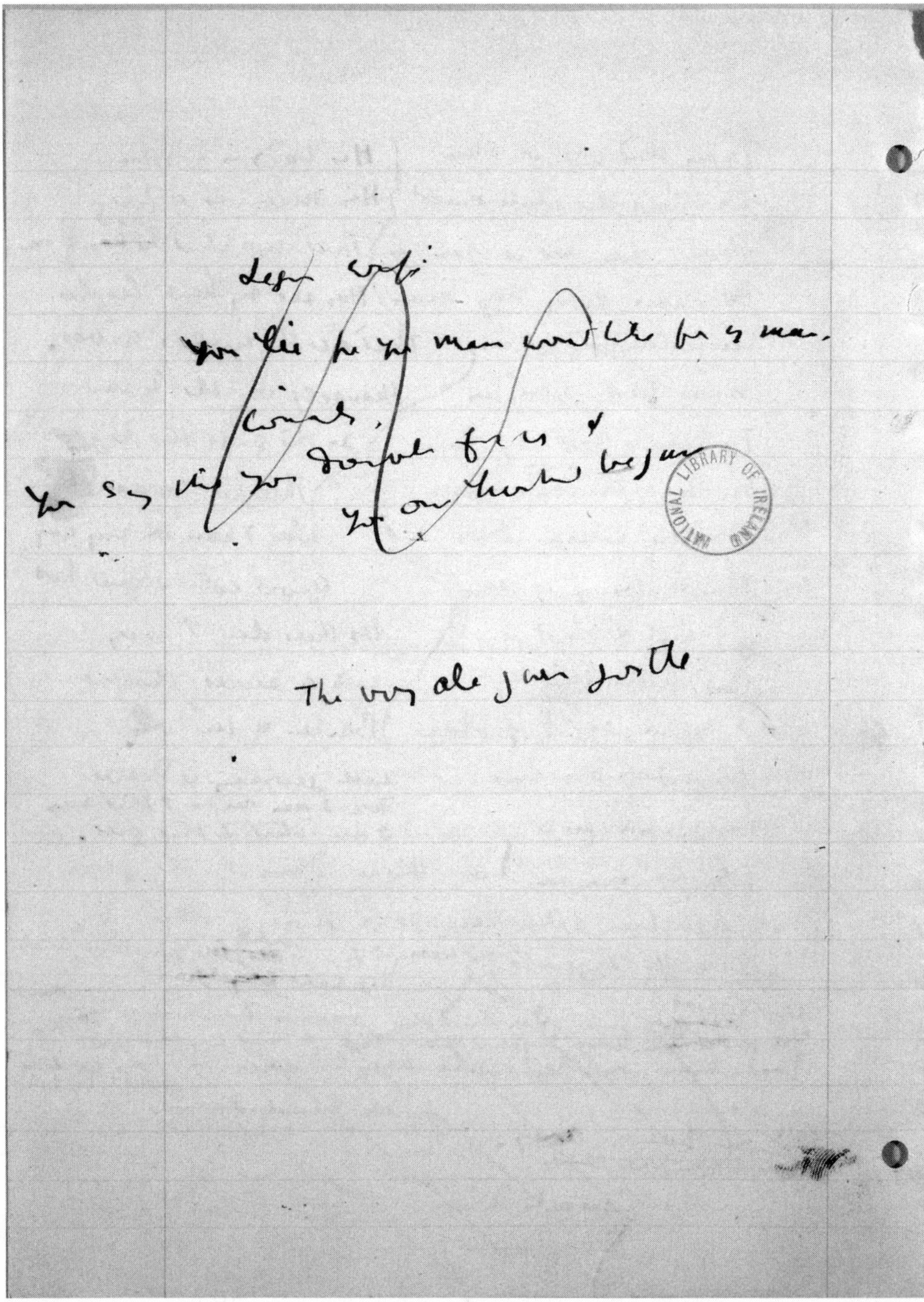

[NLI 8761, 26^{v}]

Legrs wife
1 You lie for yor man woud take from my man. [243–244]

Conals .
2 You say that you double face &
yor own husband began

3 The very ale jars jostle

1–2 A reworking of ll. 4–6 on 27^{r}.
3 Cf. l. 10 on 27^{r}.

[NLI 8761, 27r]

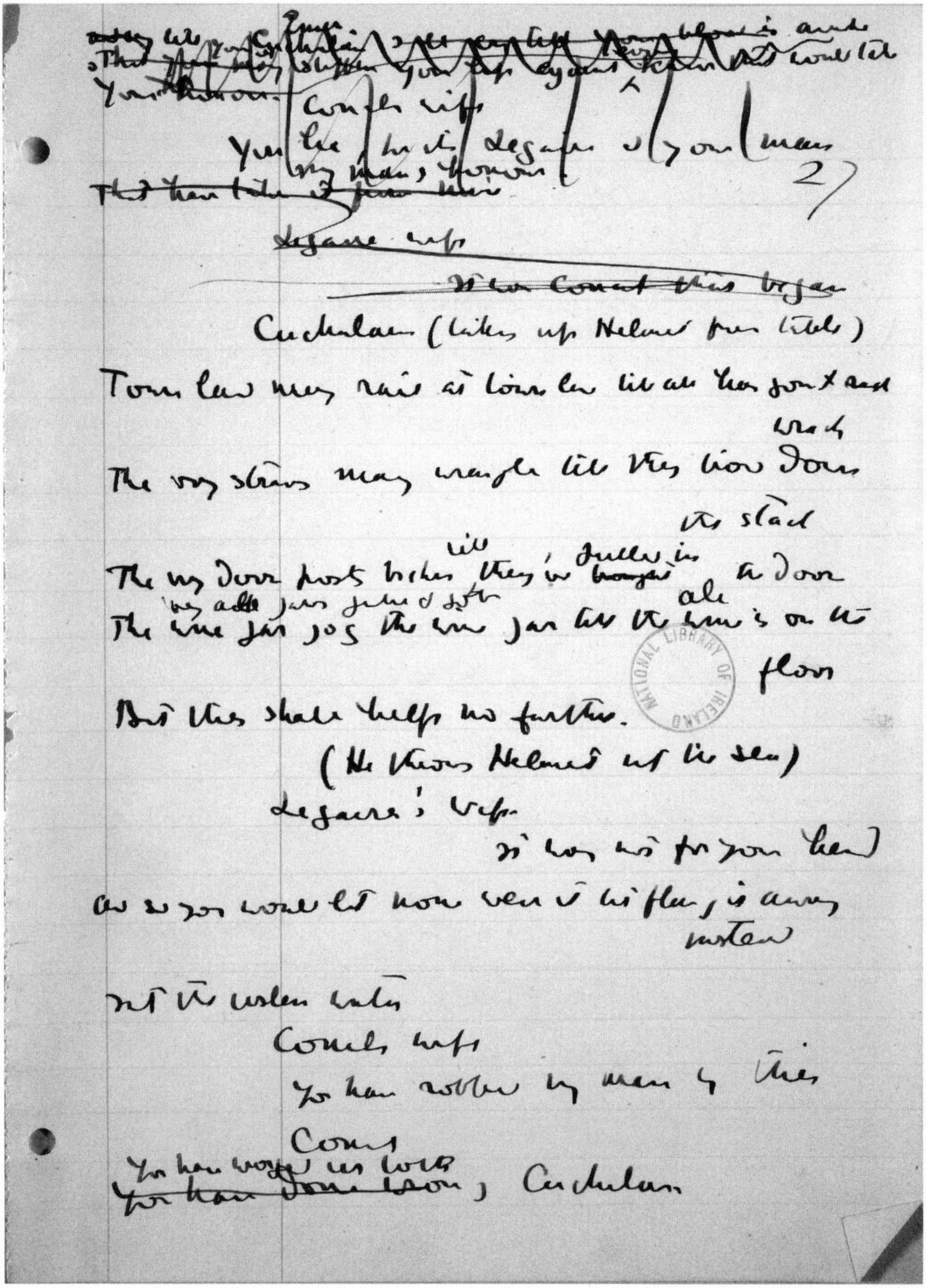
[illegible]

Conchubar ups

You have [illegible] Legaire's [illegible] of your men
my man's honour

[illegible]

Legaire ups

[illegible]

Cuchulain (takes up Helmet from table)

Town [illegible] may raise as loud as till all their joints ache

The very straws may wrangle till they blow down the stack

The very door posts bicker till they've pulled in a door

The wine jar jogs the wine jar till the ale is on the floor

But this shall help no further.

(He throws Helmet into the sea)

Legaire's wife.

It was not for your head

And so you would let none [illegible] is away

Enter the [illegible]

Conall's wife

You have robbed my man of this

Conall

You have wronged us both, Cuchulain

[NLI 8761, 27r]

27

Emer.

1 Cuchulan ~~I ll cry till your blood~~ is awake

~~and cry~~ till your bl every [241–249]

2 ^~~That you may~~ stiffen your lip against ^ Knave that would take

3 Your honour.

Conals wife

4 You lie for its Legaire & your man

my man s honour.

5 That have taken ~~it from mine~~ –

Legaire wife

6 It was Conal that began

Cuchulain (taking up Helmet from table)

7 Town land may rail at town land till all have gone to ~~rack~~

wrack

8 The very straws may wrangle till they trow down

the stack

till pulled in

9 The very door posts bicker ^ they've ~~brought~~ the door

{le

very a{ul jars jostle & jog ale

10 The wine jar jog the wine jar till the wine's on the

floor

11 But this shall help no further.

(He throws Helmet int the sea)

1–6 LAEGAIRE'S WIFE

You lie, for your man would take from my man.

CONALL'S WIFE

(to Laegaire's wife) You say that, you double-face, and your own husband began. *Cuala*

7 wrack] wrack, *Cuala*

8 they trow] they've thrown *Cuala* stack] stack. *Cuala*

9 the door] the door, *Cuala*

10 jostle & jog] jostle *Cuala* floor] floor, *Cuala*

11*sd* int] into *Cuala*

1–6 A reworking of ll. 32ff. on 26r.

[NLI 8761, 27r]

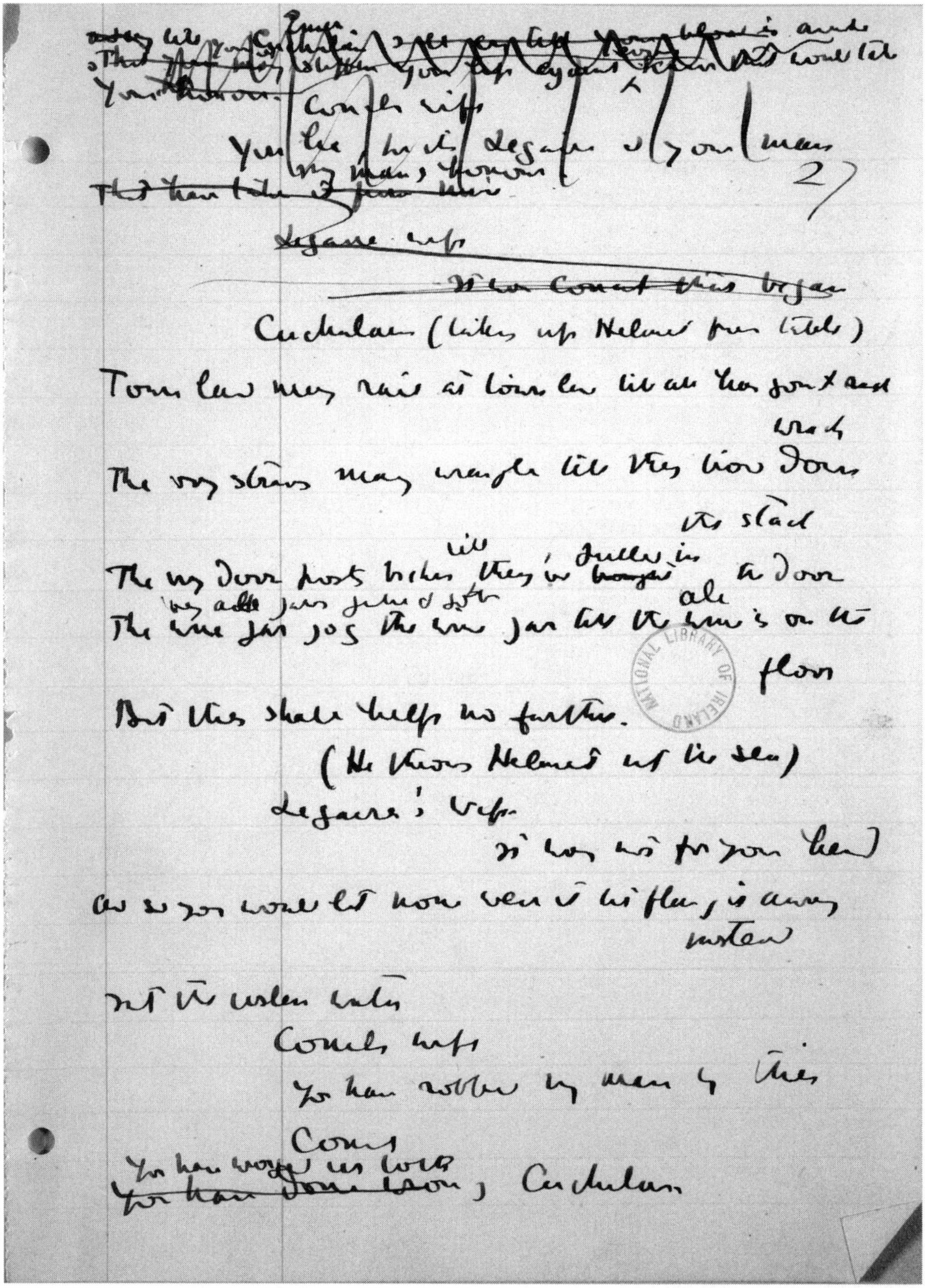
[illegible]

Conall ups

You lie [illegible] Laegaire [illegible] of your man

27

Laegaire ups

Cuchulain (takes up Helmet from table)

Town law may rail at town law till all has gone to wrack

The very stones may wrangle till they throw down the slack

The very door posts bicker till they're dulled in the door

The wine jar jog the wine jar till the ale is on the floor

But they shall help no further.

(He throws Helmet up [illegible])

Laegaire's ups

It was not for your head

And so you would let none wear it but fling it away instead

But the Ulster kings

Conall ups

You have robbed my man of this

Conns

You have wronged us both, Cuchulain

[NLI 8761, 27^{r}, continued]

Legaire's Wife.

12 It was not for your head [250–252]

13 And so you would let none wear it but fling it away
instead

14 Into the useless water

Conals wife

15 You have robbed my man by this

Conal

You have wronged us both

16 ~~You have done wrong~~ Cuchulan

---

13 instead] instead. *Cuala*

14 *lacking in Cuala*

15 But you shall answer for it, for you've robbed my man by this. *Cuala*

16 wronged us both Cuchulan] robbed us both, Cuchulain. *Cuala*

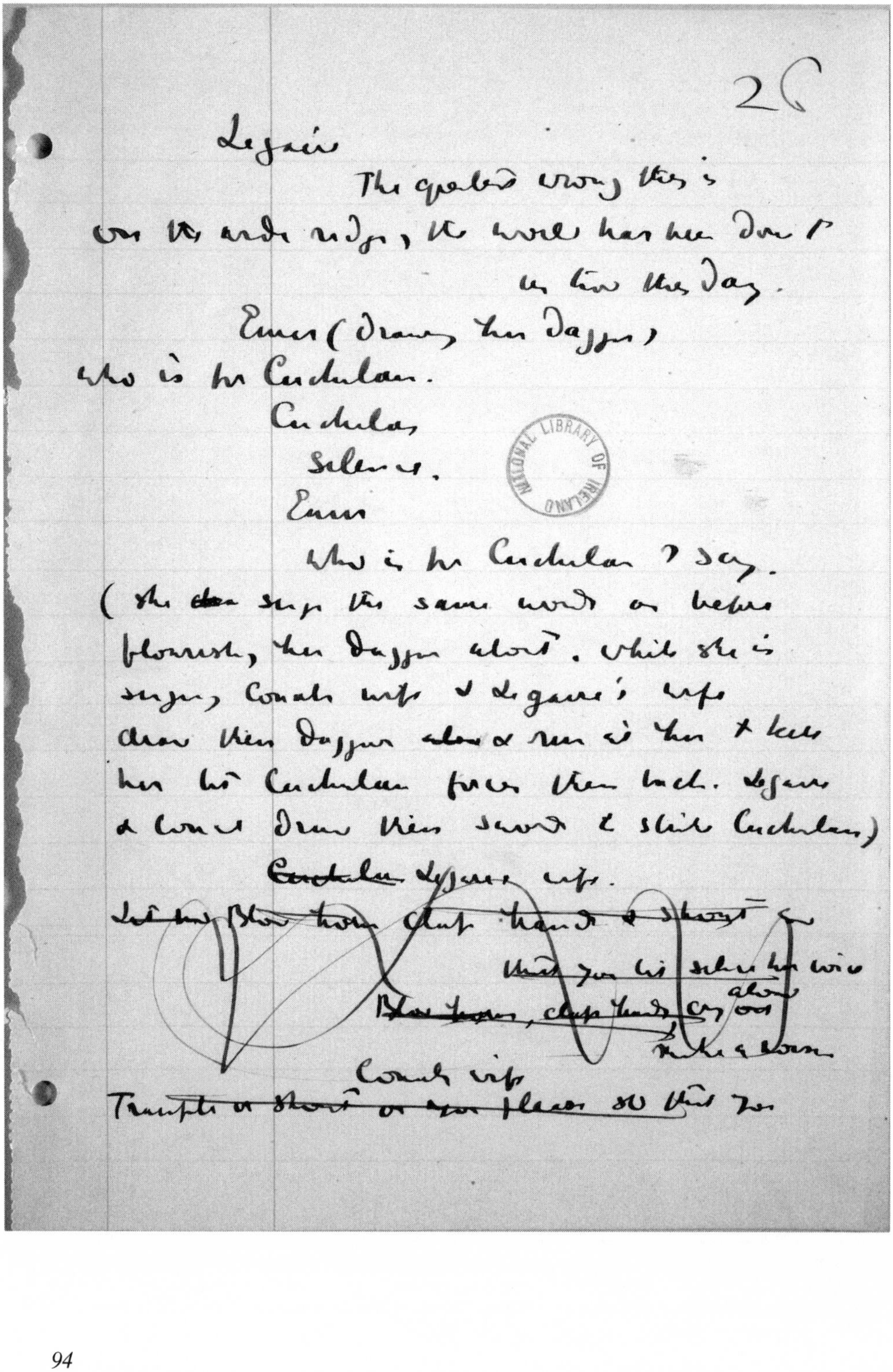
26

Legaire

The quarrels wrong this is
on the arde edge, the work has been done
up to this day.

Emer (drawing her dagger)
Who is the Cuchulain.

Cuchulain
Silence.

Emer
Who is the Cuchulain I say.

(She ~~does~~ sings the same words as before
flourishing her dagger aloft. While she is
singing, Conal's wife & Legaire's wife
draw their daggers ~~also~~ & run at her & kill
her but Cuchulain forces them back. Legaire
& Conal draw their swords & strike Cuchulain)

~~Cuchulain~~ Legaire's wife.
~~Let them Blow horns clap hands & shout~~
~~What you lie~~ silent [her wife]
~~Blow horns, clap hands,~~ cry out alone
make a noise

Conal's wife
~~Trumpets or shout or your places~~ all that you

[NLI 8761, 28[r]]

26

Legaire

1 The greatest wrong there is [252–255]

2 On the wide ridge of the world has been done to us two this day.

Emer (drawing her dagger)

3 Who is for Cuchulan.

Cuchulan

4 Silence.

Emer

5 Who is for Cuchulan I say.

(she ~~cha~~ sings the same words as before flourishing her dagger about. While she is singing Conals wife & Legaire's wife draw their daggers ~~also~~ & run at her to kill her but Cuchulan forces them back. Legaire & Conal draw their swords to strike Cuchulan.)

~~Cuchulan~~ Legare s wife.

6 ~~Let [?us]~~ Blow horn clap hand & shout so that you wil silence her voice aloud

7 Blow horns, clap hands, cry ~~out~~ make a noise

Conals wife

8 ~~Trumpet or shout as you please so that you~~

---

3 Cuchulan.] Cuchulain? *Cuala*

5 Cuchulan I say.] Cuchulain, I say?

5*sd* before flourishing] before, flourishing *Cuala* singing Conals wife & Legaire's] singing, Conall's wife and Laegaire's *Cuala* daggers also & run at her to kill her] daggers and run at her, *Cuala* Legaire & Conal] Laegaire and Conall *Cuala* Cuchulan.)] Cuchulain) *Cuala*

WBY numbered the page "26" in error for "28" (cf. the number "6" at the top of 16[r] and 26[r], above).

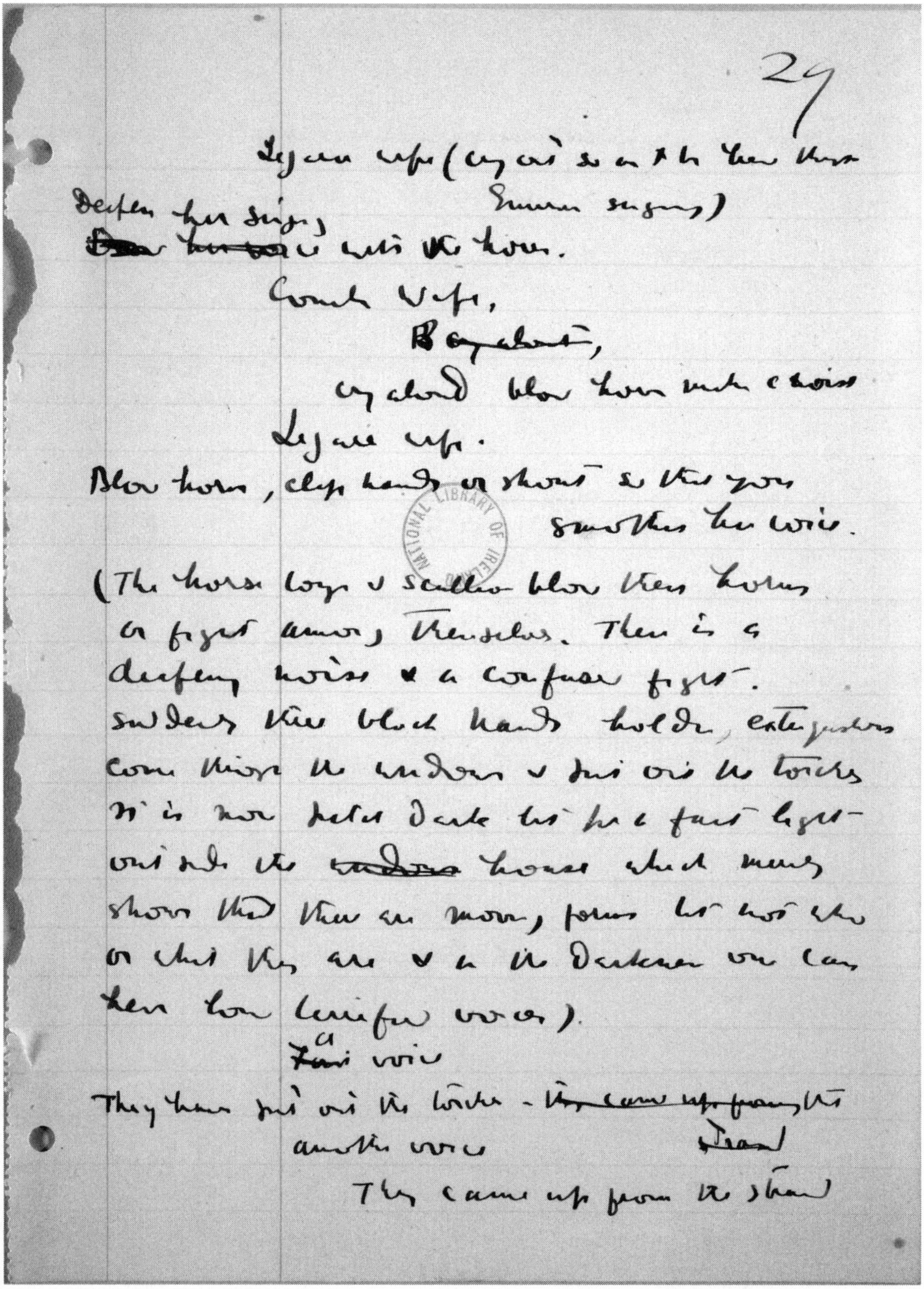
29

Legaire wife (crying out so as to drown the Emer singing)

Deafen her singing,
~~Drown her voice~~ with the horn.

Conall Wife,

Bagpipes,

cry aloud blow horn make a noise

Legaire wife.

Blow horns, clap hands or shout so that you smother her voice.

(The horse boys & scullions blow their horns or fight among themselves. There is a deafening noise & a confused fight. Suddenly three black hands holding extinguishers come through the window & put out the torches It is now pitch dark but for a faint light outside the ~~window~~ house which merely shows that there are moving forms but not who or what they are & in the darkness one can hear loud terrified voices).

a ~~Fair~~ voice

They have put out the torches – ~~they came up from the strand~~

another voice

They came up from the strand

[NLI 8761, 29r]

29

Legaire wife (cry out so as to be heard through
Emers singing)

Deafen her singing
1 ~~Drown her voice~~ with the horns. [255–259]

Conals Wife.
~~B cry about~~,
2 Cry aloud blow horns make a noise

Legaire wife.
3 Blow horns, clap hands or shout so that you smother her voice.

(The horse boys & scullions blow their horns or fight among themselves. There is a deafeng noise and a confused fight. Suddenly three black hands holding extinguishers come through the windows & put out the torches It is now pitch dark but for a faint light outside the ~~windows~~ house which merely shows that there are moving forms but not who or what they are & in the darkness one can hear low terrified voices).

A
~~Faint~~ voice
4 They have just put out the torches – ~~they came up from~~ the ~~strand~~

Another voice
5 They came up from the strand

1*sd* Legaire wife (cry out] LEGAIRE'S WIFE (crying out *Cuala* Emers] Emer's *Cuala*

1 the horns.] horns. *Cuala*

2 Cry aloud blow horns make a noise] Cry aloud! blow horns! make a noise! *Cuala*

3 clap hands or shout so] clap hands, or shout, so *Cuala*

3*sd* boys & scullions] boys and scullions *Cuala* deafeng] deafening *Cuala* Suddenly three] Suddenly, three *Cuala* holding extinguishers] *lacking in Cuala* & put out the torches] and put out the torches. *Cuala* dark but] dark, but *Cuala* forms but] forms, but *Cuala* are & in] are, and in *Cuala* voices).] voices) *Cuala*

4–5 *lacking in Cuala*

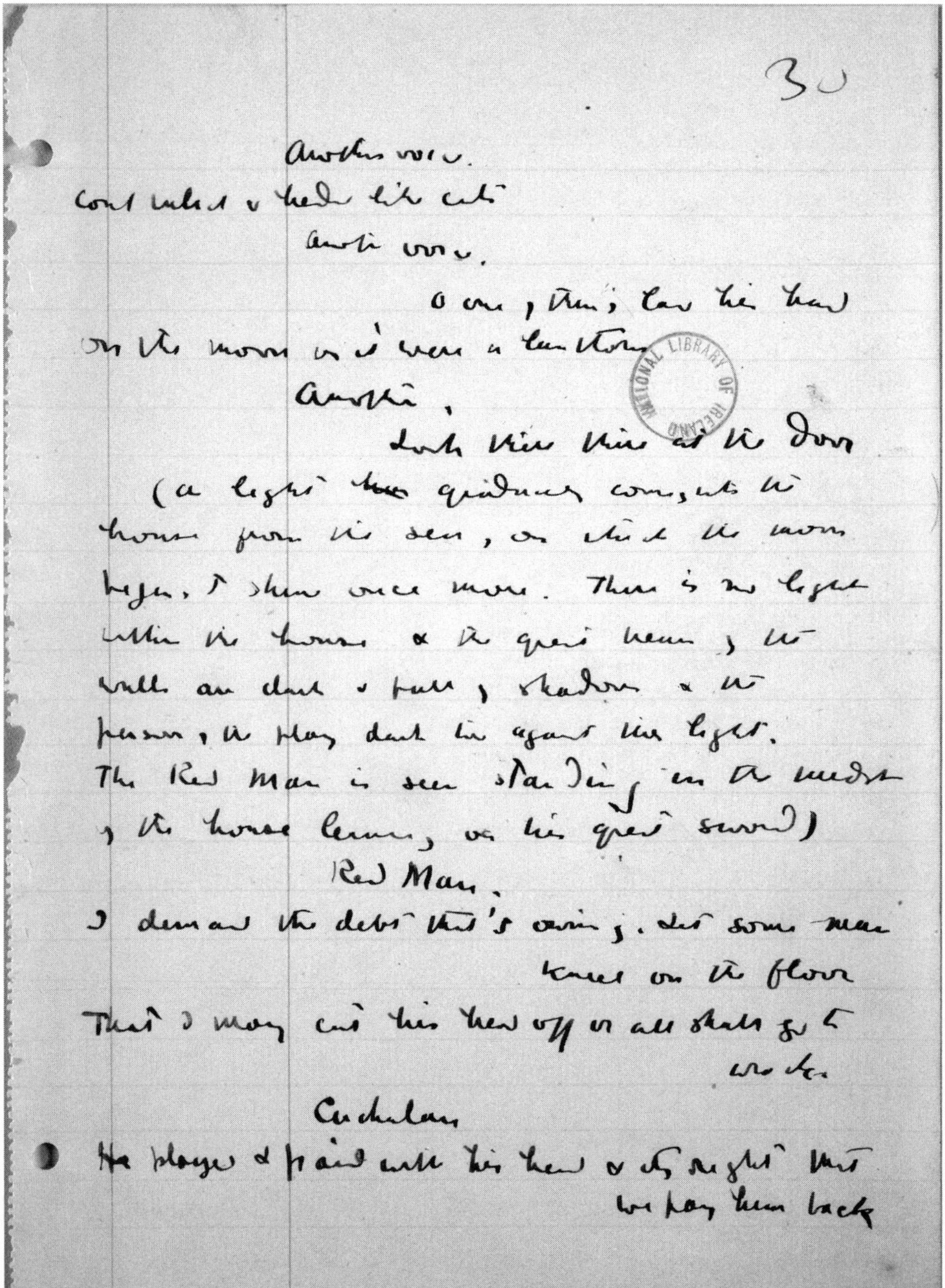
30

Another voice.
Cant what a heads like cats
Another voice.
O one of them has his head
On the moon as if it were a lantern
Another.
Look there there at the door
(A light gradually comes into the house from the sea, as though the moon began to shine once more. There is no light within the house & the great beams of the walls are dark & full of shadows & the persons of the play dark too against the light. The Red Man is seen standing in the midst of the house leaning on his great sword)
Red Man.
I demand the debt that's owing. Let some man kneel on the floor
That I may cut his head off or all shall go to wrack.
Cuchulain
He played & paid with his head & its right that we pay him back

[NLI 8761, 30^{r}]

30

Another voice.

1 Coal [?colrd] & headed like cats [257–262]

Another voice.

2 & one of them laid his hand
3 On the moon as it were a lantern

Another.

4 Look there there at the door

(A light ~~has~~ gradualy comng into the house from the sea, on which the moon begins to show once more. There is no light within the house & the great beams of the walls are dark & full of shadows & the persons of the play dark too against the light. The Red Man is seen standing in the midst of the house leaning on his great sword)

Red Man.

5 I demand the debt that's owing. Let some man kneel on the floor
6 That I may cut his head off or all shall go to wrack.

Cuchulan

7 He played & paid with his head & its right that we pay him back

---

1 Coal [?colrd] &] Coal black, and *Cuala* cats] cats. They came up over the strand. *Cuala*

2–3 And I saw one stretch to a torch and cover it with his hand. *Cuala*

4 Another sooty fellow has plucked the moon from the air. *Cuala*

4*sd* gradualy comng] gradually coming *Cuala* house & the] house, and the *Cuala* dark & full of shadows &] dark and full of shadows, and *Cuala* house leaning on his great sword] house. The black cat-headed men crouch and stand about the door. One carries the Helmet, one the great sword) *Cuala*

5 kneel on the floor] kneel down there *Cuala*

7 played & paid] played and paid *Cuala* head & its] head and it's *Cuala* back] back, *Cuala*

[NLI 8761, 31r]

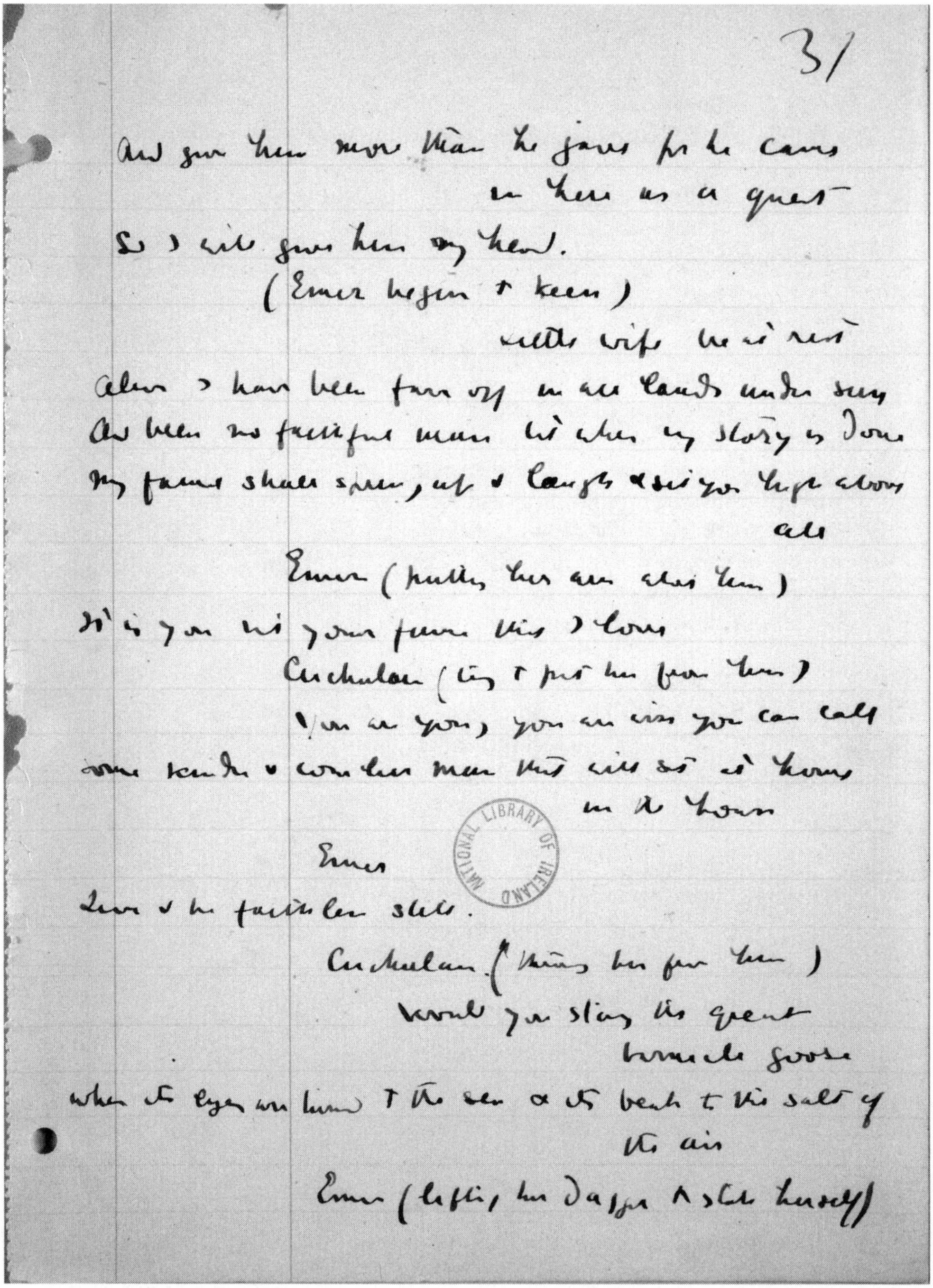
31

And give him more than he gave for he came
in here as a guest
So I will give him my head.
(Emer begins to keen)
Little wife be at rest
Alone I have been far off in all lands under sky
And been no faithful man but when my story is done
My fame shall spring up & laugh & set you high above
all
Emer (putting her arms about him)
It is you not your fame that I love
Cuchulain (trying to put her from him)
You are young, you are wise you can call
Some kinder & comelier man that will sit at home
in the house
Emer
Love & be faithless still.
Cuchulain (thrusting her from him)
Would you stay the great
barnacle goose
When its eyes are turned to the sea & its beak to the salt of
the air
Emer (lifting her dagger to stab herself)

[NLI 8761, 31r]

31

1 And give him more than he gave for he comes [263–272]
in here as a guest
2 So I will give him my head.

(Emer begins to keen)

3 Little wife be at rest
4 Alive I have been far off in all lands under sun
5 And been no faithful man but when my story is done
6 My fame shall spring up & laugh & set you high above
all

Emer (putting her arm about him)
7 It is you not your fame that I love

Cuchulan (tries to put her from him)
8 You are young you are wise you can call
9 Some kinder & comelier man that will sit at home
in the house

Emer
10 Live and be faithless still.

Cuchulan (throwing her from him)
11 Would you slay the great
barnacle goose
13 When its eyes are turned to the sea & its beak to the salt of
the air

Emer (lifting her dagger to stab herself)

---

1 gave for] gave, for *Cuala* guest] guest, *Cuala*
3 wife be] wife, little wife, be *Cuala* rest] rest. *Cuala*
4 sun] sun, *Cuala*
5 man but] man, but *Cuala*
6 up & laugh & set] up and laugh, and set *Cuala* all] all. *Cuala*
7*sd* arm] arms *Cuala*
7 love] love. *Cuala*
8 young you are wise you] young, you are wise, you *Cuala*
9 & comelier] and comlier *Cuala* house] house. *Cuala*
10 Live and] Live, and *Cuala*
11 barnacle goose] barnacle-goose *Cuala*
12 sea & its] sea and its *Cuala* air] air? *Cuala*

---

3 The "L" of the first "Little" is very lightly stroked but is definitely a capital letter (cf. "Live" in l. 10).

7*sd* The spelling "arm" is also the reading in the text of the play that was printed in *The Forum* (New York), September 1911. In 1930 *The Forum* became *The Century*.

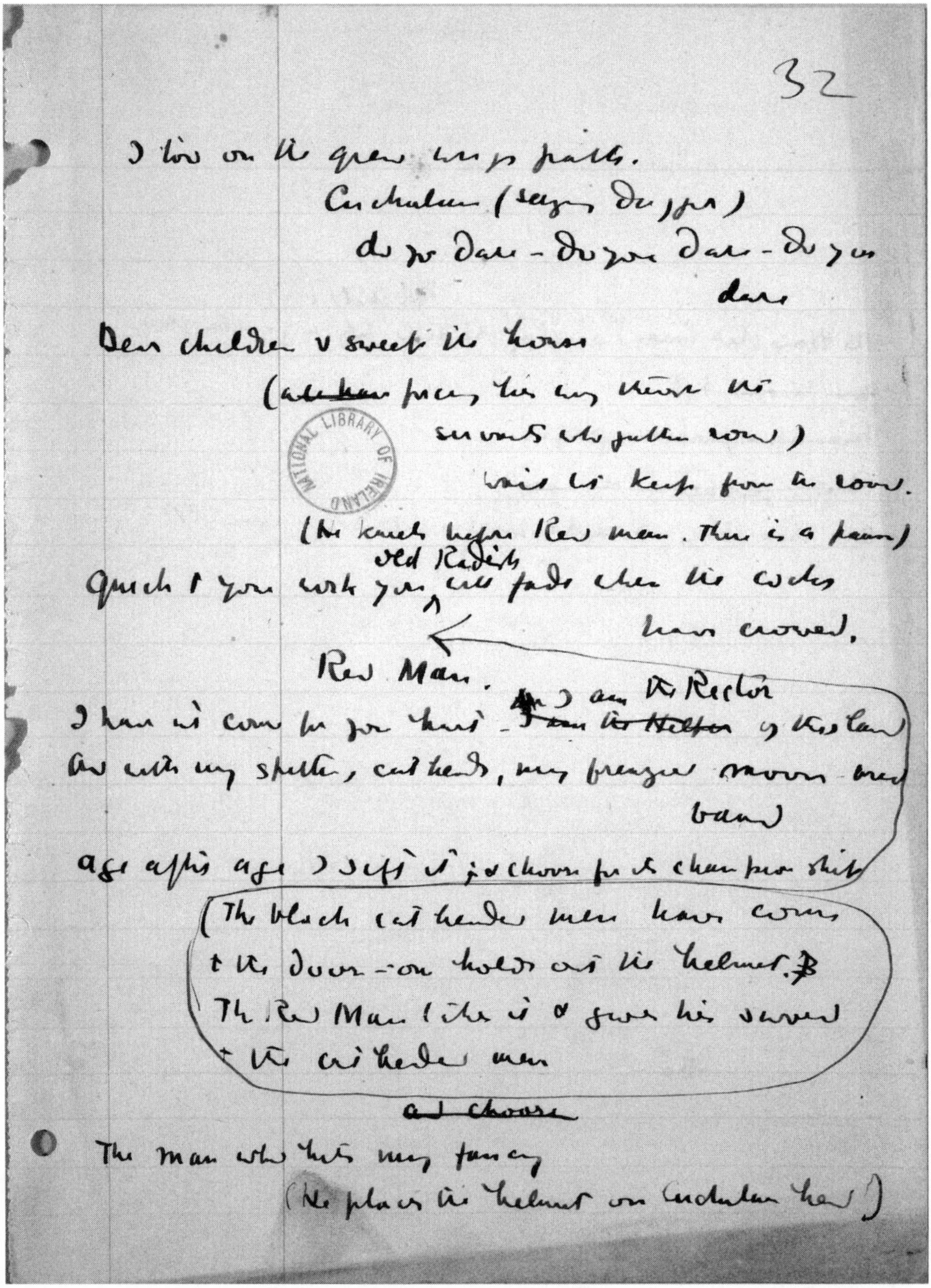
32

I live on the green wings path.
Cuchulain (seizing dagger)
do you dare - do you dare - do you dare

Dear children & sweet the horses
(~~ale-house~~ pieces, his ... throws the servants who gather round)
wait to keep from the room.
(He kneels before Red man. There is a pause)
Quick & you work yes, old Radish all fade when the cocks have crowed.

Red Man.
I have not come for your hurt. ~~I am the Helper~~ I am the Rector of this land
And with my spitter, cat heads, my frenzied moon-bred band
age after age I sift it & choose for its championship

(The black cat headed men have come to the door - one holds out the helmet. The Red Man takes it & gives his sword to the cat headed men

~~and choose~~

The man who hits my fancy
(He places the helmet on Cuchulain head)

1 The printer's error "winds" was first corrected to "wing's" in *Plays for an Irish Theatre* in 1911.

[NLI 8761, 32r]

32

1 I too on the grey wings path. [272–278]

Cuchulan (seizing dagger)

2 Do you dare – do you dare – do you dare

3 Bear children & sweep the house

(~~all have~~ forcing his way through the servants who gather round)

4 Wail but keep from the road.

(He kneels before Red Man. There is a pause)

Old Radish

5 Quick to your work you ^ will fade when the cocks have crowed.

Red Man.

~~am~~ I am the Rector

6 I have not come for your hurt – ~~I am the Helper~~ of this land

7 And with my spitting cat heads, my frenzied moon bred band

8 Age after age I sift it; & choose for its champion ship

(The black cat headed men have come to the door – one holds out the helmet. ~~)~~ The Red Man takes it & gives his sword to the cat headed men

~~and choose~~

9 The man who hits my fancy

(He places the helmet on Cuchulan head)

---

1 I too] I, too, *Cuala* wings] winds *Cuala*
2 Do you dare, do you dare, do you dare. *Cuala*
3 children & sweep] children and sweep *Cuala* house] house. *Cuala*
4 Wail but] Wail, but *Cuala* road.] road *Cuala*
4*sd* He] he *Cuala*
5 you Old Radish] old Radish, you *Cuala*
5*sd* (A black cat-headed man holds out the Helmet. The Red Man takes it) *Cuala*
6 hurt—I am] hurt, I am *Cuala* land] land, *Cuala*
7 spitting cat] spitting-cat *Cuala* moon bred] moon-bred *Cuala* band] band, *Cuala*
8 sift it; & choose] sift it, and choose *Cuala* champion ship] champion-ship *Cuala*
8*sd* *see 5sd, above*
9 fancy] fancy. *Cuala*
9*sd* helmet] Helmet *Cuala* Cuchulan] Cuchulain's *Cuala*

[NLI 8761, 32v]

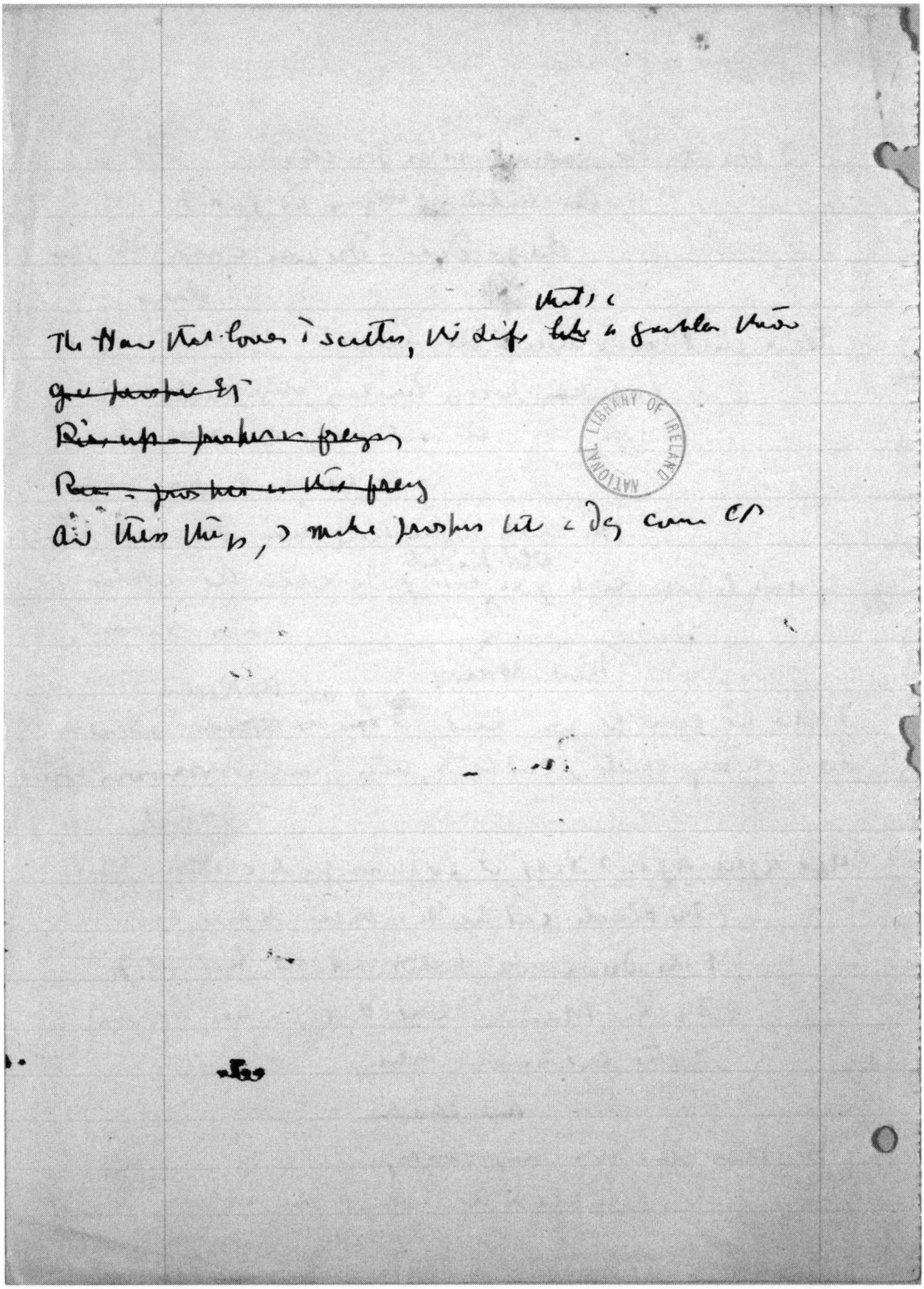

[NLI 8761, 32^{v}]

that s a
The Hand that loves to scatter, the Life ~~like~~ a gambler throw [281–282]
~~Go & prosper Et~~
~~Rise up – prosper in frenzy~~
~~Rise –prosper in this frenzy~~
And these things, I make prosper till a day come Et

1–5 A reworking of ll. 4–5 on 33^{r}. See the *apparatus criticus* on p. 107, below.
2, 5 For "Et" read "Etc."

[NLI 8761, 33^{r}]

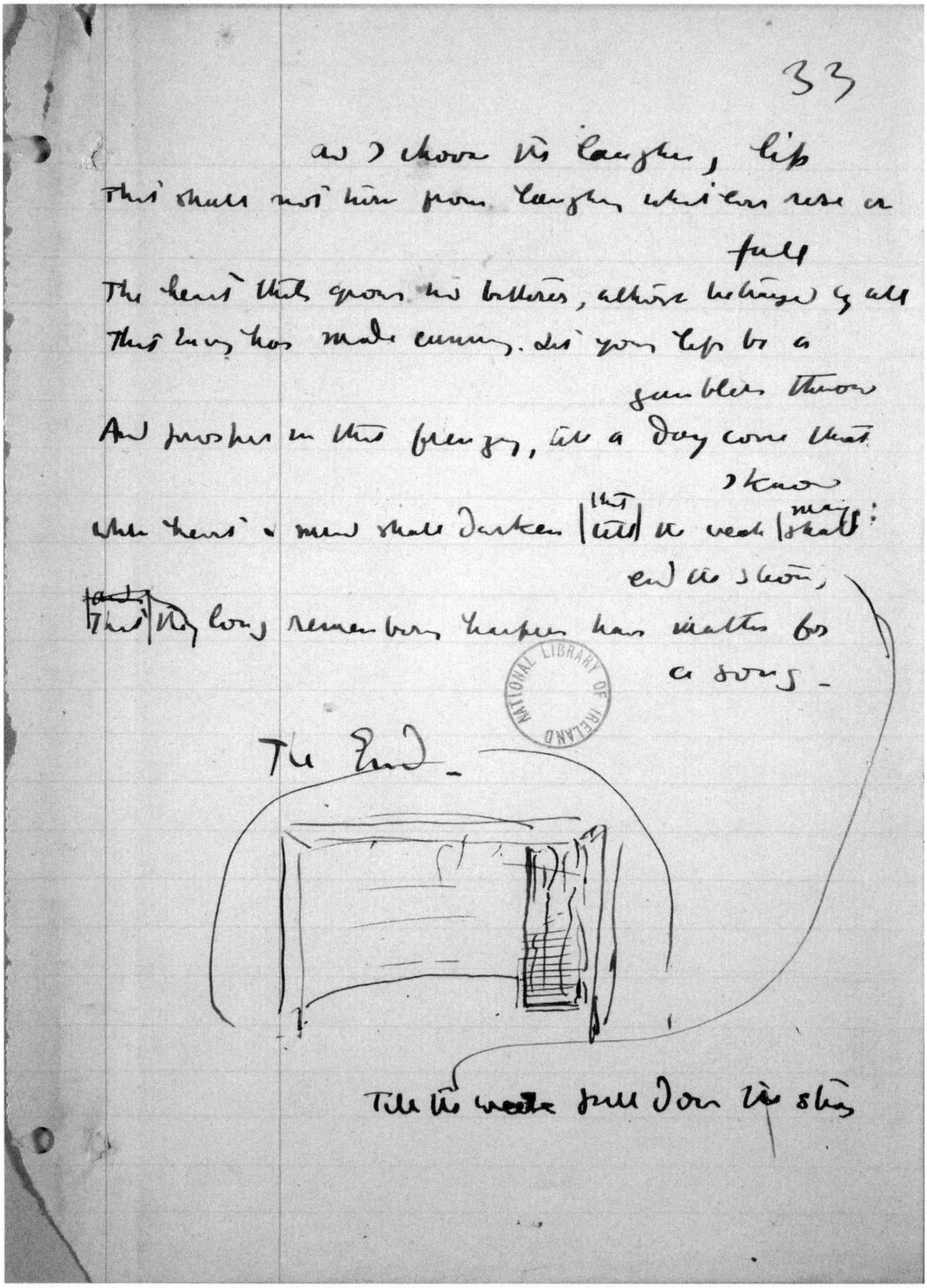
33

and I choose the laughing lip
That shall not turn from laughing, whatever rise or fall
The heart that grows no bitterer, although betrayed by all
That luck has made cunning. Set your lips to a gambler's throw
And prosper in that frenzy, till a day come that I know
When heart and mind shall darken that the weak may end the strong,
~~And~~ That the long remembering harpers have matter for a song —

The End —

Till the [illegible] fall down the stage

The sketch for the stage design resembles the actual stage as shown in the contemporary photographs of "Scenes from The Golden Helmet," with timber walls and a door at right rear (see Appendix B, pp. 146–147, below).

[NLI 8761, 33r]

33

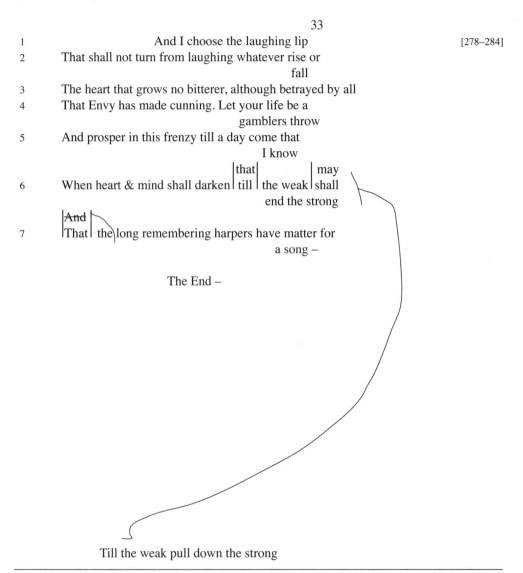

1 And I choose the laughing lip [278–284]
2 That shall not turn from laughing whatever rise or
fall
3 The heart that grows no bitterer, although betrayed by all
4 That Envy has made cunning. Let your life be a
gamblers throw
5 And prosper in this frenzy till a day come that
I know
|that| |may
6 When heart & mind shall darken | till | the weak | shall
end the strong
|~~And~~|
7 |That| the long remembering harpers have matter for
a song –

The End –

Till the weak pull down the strong

---

1 choose] chose *Cuala*
2 fall] fall, *Cuala*
3 bitterer,] bitterer *Cuala* all] all, *Cuala*
4 The hand that loves to scatter, the life like a gambler's throw; *Cuala*
5 And prosper in this frenzy] And these things I make prosper, *Cuala* know] know, *Cuala*
6 heart & mind] heart and mind *Cuala* till the weak shall] that the weak may *Cuala* strong] strong, *Cuala*
7 That the long] And the long *Cuala* a song –] their song. *Cuala*
7+ The End – *lacking Cuala*

6, 7 The vertical lines mark alternative readings. A further alternative for l. 6 appears at the foot. In l. 7 WBY apparently suggested the reading "And long remembering harpers . . . " and then restored the original reading.

The Green Helmet (An Heroic Farce). Proof Pages of *Collected Plays* (1934). BL(2)

As he did with much of his work, Yeats revisited *The Green Helmet* in the 1930s in the course of preparing the never-published Macmillan Edition de Luxe. As the de Luxe edition was repeatedly delayed during the first half of the decade, Macmillan agreed to publish a single-volume *Collected Plays* in 1934 as a kind of intermediate measure. By that time, Yeats had grown to trust Thomas Mark, his editor at Macmillan, to make corrections to proofs in matters of spelling, typesetting, and so on. Often, as is the case with the proofs transcribed here, both Mark and Yeats corrected proofs, occasionally engaging in a kind of marginal dialogue when Mark had questions or suggestions. It is these proofs that are transcribed in the following pages

Most of the marginal annotation here is in Mark's hand. However, Yeats made some substantial changes to the text of the play during the correction of these proofs. In other places, he responds to Mark's questions and suggestions. In this transcription, Mark's annotations are represented in italics, while Yeats's are in roman face.

Later in the 1930s, after the publication of *Collected Plays*, Thomas Mark and George Yeats returned to the proofs for the Edition de Luxe, incorporating the substantive changes Yeats made for *Collected Plays*. The changes made in the Edition de Luxe proofs and in *Collected Plays* (1934) are included in the *apparatus criticus*.

[BL(2)]

[115r]

THE GREEN HEMLET tr/

(An Heroic Farce)

PERSONS IN THE PLAY

Laegaire	**Laegaire's Wife**
Conall	**Conall's Wife**
Cuchulain	**Laeg,** ***Cuchulain's chariot-driver***
Red Man, ***a Spirit***	**Stable Boys and Scullions**
Emer	**Black Men, etc.**

A house made of logs. There are two windows at the back and a door which cuts off one of the corners of the room. Through the door one can see low rocks which make the ground Outside higher than it is within, and beyond the rocks a misty moon-lit sea. Through the windows one can see nothing but the sea. There is a great chair at the opposite side to the door, and in front of it a table with cups and a flagon of ale. Here and there are stools.

At the Abbey Theatre the house is orange red and the chairs and tables and flagons black, with a slight purple tinge which is not clearly distinguishable from the black. The rocks are black with a few green touches. The sea is green and luminous, and all the characters except the Red Man and the Black Men are dressed in various shades of green, one or two with touches of purple that look nearly black. The Black Men all wear dark purple and have eared caps, and at the end their eyes should look green from the reflected light of the sea. The Red Man is altogether in red. He is very tall, and his height increased by horns on the Green Helmet. The effect is intentionally violent and startling.

~~223~~

---

found in BL(2) *transcribed above and below*
NLI 30,006/4
BL(1)
published *CPl* (1934)

---

title THE GREEN HEMLET] THE GREEN HELMET *NLI 30,006/4, CPl* THE GREEN HELMET, *footnote added reading* See note at end of volume *BL(1)*

persons in the play Conall's Wife *lacking*; *a marginal note inserts* (CONALL'S WIFE?) / (~~She has a speaking / part~~) *NLI 30,006/4* Stable] Horse *del and rev to* STABLE *NLI 30,006/4* Laegaire] Laegaire *rev to* Laegaire (pronounced Leary) *BL(1)*

9 orange red *rev to* orange-red *NLI 30,006/4 and BL(1)*

[115^{v}]

~~224~~ THE GREEN HELMET

Laegaire. **What is that? I had thought that I saw, though** [1–15]
but in the wink of an eye,
Connacht? **A cat-headed man out of Connaught go pacing and**
spitting by;
But that could not be.
Conall. **You have dreamed it—there's nothing out there**
I killed them all before daybreak—I hoked them out ^ of/?
their lair;
I cut off a hundred head with a single stroke of my
sword,
And then I danced on their graves and carried away
their hoard.
Laegaire. **Does anything stir on the sea?**
Conall. **Not even a fish or a gull:**
I can see for a mile or two, now that the moon's at
the full. [*A distant shout.*
Laegaire. **Ah—there—there is some one who calls us.**
Conall. **But from the landward side,**
And we have nothing to fear that has not come up
from the tide;
The rocks and the bushes cover whoever made that
noise,
But the land will do us no harm.
Laegaire. **It was like Cuchulain's voice.**
Conall. **But that's an impossible thing.**
Laegaire. **An impossible thing indeed.**
Conall. **For he will never come home, he has all that**
he could need
In that high windy Scotland—good luck in all that he
does.

---

23 Connaught *rev to* Connacht *NLI 30,006/4* Connacht *CPl*
26 out there] out there *rev to* out there. *BL(1)*
27–28 out / their] out / of their *CPl*

21ff. Numbers in brackets at the right are the corresponding line numbers in *VPl*, pp. 422–453.

[BL(2)]

[116^{r}]

THE GREEN HELMET ~~225~~

Here neighbour wars on neighbour, and why there [16–30]
is no man knows,
And if a man is lucky all wish his luck away,
And take his good name from him between a day
and a day.
***Laegaire*. I would he'd come for all that, and make his**
young wife know
That though she may be his wife, she has no right
to go
Before your wife and my wife, as she would have
done last night
Had they not caught at her dress, and pulled her as
was right;
And she makes light of us though our wives do all
that they can.
She spreads her tail like a peacock and praises none
but her man.
***Conall.* A man in a long green cloak that covers him**
up to the chin
Comes down through the rocks and hazels.
***Laegaire.* Cry out that he cannot come in.**
***Conall.* He must look for his dinner elsewhere, for no**
one alive shall stop
Where a shame must alight on us two before the
dawn is up.
***Laegaire.* No man on the ridge of the world must ever**
know that but us two.
***Conall [outside door]*. Go away, go away, go away.**
***Young Man [outside door]*. I will go when the night is**
through

---

51 neighbour, and] neighbor and *rev to* neighbour, and *NLI 30,006/4*

[116v]

~~226~~ THE GREEN HELMET

And I have eaten and slept and drunk to my heart's [31–44]
delight.
Conall. A law had been made that none shall sleep in
this house to-night.
Young Man. Who made that law?
Conall. We made it, and who has so good a right?
Who else has to keep the house from the Shape-
Changers till day?
Young Man. Then I will unmake the law, so get you
out of the way.
[*He pushes past Conall and goes into the house.*
Conall. I thought no man living could have pushed me
from the door,
Nor could any living man do it but for the dip in
the floor;
And had I been rightly ready there's no man living
could do it,
Dip or no dip.
Laegaire. Go out—if you have your wits, go out,
A stone's throw further on you will find a big house
where
Our wives will give you supper, and you'll sleep
sounder there,
For it's a luckier house.
Young Man. I'll eat and sleep where I will.
Laegaire. Go out or I will make you.
*Young Man [forcing up Laegaire's arm, passing him and
putting his shield on the wall over the chair].* Not till
I have drunk my fill,
But may some dog defend me, for a cat of wonder's
up.

---

93 door,] door *rev to* door, *NLI 30,006/4*
110 defend me,] defend me *rev to* defend me, *NLI 30,006/4*

[BL(2)]

[117r]

Laegaire and Conall are there the flagon full to the [45–58]
top,
And the cups—
Laegaire. It is Cuchulain.
Cuchulain. The cups are dry as a bone.
[*He sits on chair and drinks.*
Conall. Go into Scotland again, or where you will, but
begone
From this unlucky country that was made when the
devil spat. D
Cuchulain. If I lived here a hundred years, could a worse
thing come than that
Laegaire and Conall should know me and bid me
begone to my face?
Conall. We bid you begone from a house that has fallen
on shame and disgrace.
Cuchulain. I am losing patience, Conall—I find you
stuffed with pride,
The flagon full to the brim, the front door standing
wide;
You'd put me off with words, but the whole thing's
plain enough,
You are waiting for some message to bring you to
war or love
In that old secret country beyond the wool-white
waves,
Or it may be down beneath them in foam-bewildered caves
Where nine forsaken sea-queens fling shuttles to and
fro;

121 devil] Devil *CPl*
140 sea-queens] sea queens *rev to* sea-queens *NLI 30,006/4*

[117v]

~~228~~ THE GREEN HELMET

But beyond them, or beneath them, whether you will [59–74]
or no,
I am going too.
Laegaire. Better tell it all out to the end;
He was born to luck in the cradle, his good luck may
amend
The bad luck we were born to.
Conall. I'll lay the whole thing bare.
You saw the luck that he had when he pushed in
past me there.
Does anything stir on the sea?
Laegaire. Not even a fish or a gull.
Conall. You were gone but a little while. We were
there and the ale-cup full.
We were half drunk and merry, and midnight on
the stroke,
When a wide, high man came in with a red foxy
cloak,
With half-shut foxy eyes and a great laughing mouth,
And he said, when we bid him drink, that he had so
great a drouth
He could drink the sea.
Cuchulain. I thought he had come for one of you
Connacht? Out of some Connaught rath, and would lap up
milk and mew;
But if he so loved water I have the tale awry.
Conall. You would not be so merry if he were standing
by,
For when we had sung or danced as he were our next
of kin

---

161 he said,] he said *rev to* he said, *NLI 30,006/4*
165 Connaught] Connaught *rev to* Connacht *NLI 30,006/4* Connacht *CPl*

[BL(2)]

[118r]

He promised to show us a game, the best that ever [75–89]
had been;
And when we had asked what game, he answered,
'Why, whip off my head!
Then one of you two stoop down, and I'll whip off
his', he said.
'A head for a head', he said, 'that is the game that I
play'.
***Cuchulain*. How could he whip off a head when his**
own had been whipped away?
***Conall*. We told him it over and over, and that ale had**
fuddled his wit,
But he stood and laughed at us there, as though his
sides would split,
Till I could stand it no longer, and whipped off his
head at a blow,
Being mad that he did not answer, and more at his
laughing so,
And there on the ground where it fell it went on
laughing at me.
***Laegaire*. Till he took it up in his hands—**
***Conall*. And splashed himself into the sea.**
***Cuchulain*. I have imagined as good when I've been as**
deep in the cup.
***Laegaire*. You never did.**
***Cuchulain*. And believed it.**
***Conall*. Cuchulain, when will you stop**
Boasting of your great deeds and weighing yourself
with us two,
And crying out to the world, whatever we say or do,

---

200 world, whatever] world whetever *rev to* world, whatever *NLI 30,006/4*

[118v]

~~230~~ **THE GREEN HELMET**

[90–104]

That you've said or done a better?—Nor is it a
drunkard's tale,
Though we said to ourselves at first that it all came
out of the ale,
And thinking that if we told it we should be a
laughing-stock
Swore we should keep it secret.
Laegaire. **But twelve months upon the clock.** —/
Conall. **A twelvemonth from the first time.** —/
Laegaire. **And the jug full up to the brim:**
For we had been put from our drinking by the very
thought of him. —/
Conall. **We stood as we're standing now.** —/
Laegaire. **The horns were as empty** —/
Conall. **When**
He ran up out of the sea with his head on his
shoulders again.
Cuchulain. **Why this is a tale worth telling.**
Conall. **And he called for his debt and his right,**
And said that the land was disgraced because of us
two from that night
If we did not pay him his debt.
Laegaire. **What is there to be said**
When a man with a right to get it has come to ask
for your head?
Conall. **If you had been sitting there you had been**
silent like us.
Laegaire. **He said that in twelve months more he would**
come again to this house
And ask his debt again. Twelve months are up to-day.

Would dashes look better than full stops for interrupted speech?

yes

---

208 clock] clock. *rev to* clock— *NLI 30,006/4* clock— *CPl*
209 time.] time. *rev to* time— *NLI 30,006/4* time— *CPl*
212 him.] him. *rev to* him— *NLI 30,006/4* him— *CPl*
213 now.] now. *rev to* now— *NLI 30,006/4* now— *CPl*
214 empty] empty, *rev to* empty— *NLI 30,006/4* empty— *CPl*

[BL(2)]

[119r]

THE GREEN HELMET ~~231~~

Conall. **He would have followed after if we had run away.** [105–117]
Laegaire. **Will he tell every mother's son that we have broken our word?**
Cuchulain. **Whether he does or does not, we'll drive him out with the sword,**
And take his life in the bargain if he but dare to scoff.
Conall. **How can you fight with a head that laughs when you've whipped it off?**
Laegaire. **Or a man that can pick it up and carry it out in his hand?**
Conall. **He is coming now, there's a splash and a rumble along the strand**
As when he came last.
Cuchulain. **Come, and put all your backs to the door.**
[*A tall red-headed, red-cloaked man stands upon the threshold against the misty green of the sea; the ground, higher without than within the house, makes him seem taller even than he is. He leans upon a great two-handed sword.*
Laegaire. **It is too late to shut it, for there he stands once more**
And laughs like the sea.
Cuchulain. **Old herring—You whip off heads! Why, then,**
Whip off your own, for it seems you can clap it on again.
Or else go down in the sea, go down in the sea, I say,
Find that old juggler Manannan and whip his head away;

247 tall] tall, *rev to* tall *NLI 30,006/4*
256 then,] then *rev to* then, *NLI 30,006/4*

[119v]

~~232~~ THE GREEN HELMET

Or the Red Man of the Boyne, for they are of your [118–134]
own sort,
Or if the waves have vexed you and you would find a
sport
Of a more Irish fashion, go fight without a rest
A caterwauling phantom among the winds of the
W west.
I But what are you waiting for? into the water, I say!
If there's no sword can harm you, I've an older trick
to play,
An old five-fingered trick to tumble you out of the
place;
I am Sualtim's son, Cuchulain—What, do you laugh
in my face?
Red Man. So you too think me in earnest in wagering
poll for poll!
A drinking joke and a gibe and a juggler's feat, that
is all,
To make the time go quickly—for I am the drinker's
friend,
The kindest of all Shape-Changers from here to the
world's end,
The best of all tipsy companions. And now I bring
you a gift:
I will lay I there on the ground for the best of you
all to lift [*He lays his Helmet on the ground.*
And wear upon his own head, and choose for yourselves the best.
O, Laegaire and Conall are brave, but they were
afraid of my jest.
Well, maybe I jest too grimly when the ale is in the
cup.

---

268 west] West *CPl*
269 into] Into *CPl* water,] water *rev to* water, *NLI 30,006/4*
274 son,] son *rev to* son, *NLI 30,006/4* What,] what, *rev to* What, *NLI 30,006/4*
287 lift] lift, *rev to* lift *NLI 30,006/4*
290 O,] Oh, *rev to* O, *NLI 30,006/4*

There, I'm forgiven now—

[*Then in a more solemn voice as he goes out.*

Let the bravest take it up.

[*Conall takes up Helmet and gazes at it with delight.*

Laegaire [*singing, with a swaggering stride*].

Laegaire is best;
Between water and hill,
He fought in the West
With cat-heads, until
At the break of day
All fell by his sword,
And he carried away
Their hidden hoard.

[*He seizes the Helmet.*

Conall. ~~Give it me~~, for what did you find in the bag X Short line?
But the straw and the broken delf and the bits of dirty rag
You'd taken for good money?

Cuchulain. No, no, but give it me.

[*He takes Helmet.*

Conall. The Helmet's mine or Laegaire's—you're the youngest of us three.

Cuchulain [*filling Helmet with ale*]. I did not take it to keep it—the Red Man gave it for one,
But I shall give it to all—to all of us three or to none;
That if as you look upon it—we will pass it to and fro,
And time and time about, drink out of it and so
Stroke into peace this cat that has come to take our lives.

S/

Laegaire, this Helmet is mine,

[BL(2), 120r]

THE GREEN HELMET ~~233~~

There, I'm forgiven now— [135–152]
[Then in a more solemn voice as he goes out.
Let the bravest take it up.
[Conall takes up Helmet and gazes at it with delight.
Laegaire **[*singing, with a swaggering stride*].**
Laegaire is best;
Between water and hill,
He fought in the West
With cat-heads, until
At the break of day
All fell by his sword,
And he carried away
Their hidden hoard.
[He seizes the Helmet.
Conall. **~~Give it to me~~, for what did you find in the bag** Short line?
But the straw and the broken delf and the bits of dirty rag
You'd taken for good money?
Cuchulain. **No, no, but give it me.**
[He takes Helmet.
Conall. **The Helmet's mine or Laegaire's—you're the youngest of us three.**
Cuchulain **[filling Helmet with ale]. I did not take it to keep it—the Red Man gave it for one,**
But I shall give it to all—to all of us three or to none;
s **That it as you look upon it—we will pass it to and fro,**
And time and time about, drink out of it and so
Stroke into peace this cat that has come to take our lives.

Laegaire, this Helmet is mine,

---

301 West] west *rev to* West *NLI 30,006/4*
302 cat-heads] cat heads *rev to* cat-heads *NLI 30,006/4*
308 ~~Give it to me~~,] Laegaire, that Helmet is mine, *CPl*
320 it] is *CPl*

~~234~~ THE GREEN HELMET

Now it is purring again, and now I drink to your wives,
And I drink to Emer, my wife.
[A great noise without and shouting.
Why, what in God's name is that noise?

Conall. What else but the charioteers and the kitchen and stable boys
Shouting against each other, and the worst of all is your own,
That chariot-driver, Laeg, and they'll keep it up till the dawn,
And there's not a man in the house that will close his eyes to-night,
Or be able to keep them from it, or know what set them to fight. *[A noise of horns without.*
There, do you hear them now? Such hatred has each for each
They have taken the hunting-horns to drown one another's speech
For fear the truth may prevail.—Here's your good health and long life
And, though she be quarrelsome, good health to Emer, your wife.

[The Charioteers, Stable Boys, and Scullions come running in. They carry great horns, ladles, and the like.

and other ~~[illegible]~~ instruments

~~Laegaire~~. I am Laeg, Cuchulain's driver, and my master's cock of the yard.

Another. Conall would scatter his feathers.
[Confused murmurs.

What "Another" means — Charioteer or Stable Boy

Laegaire [to Cuchulain]. No use, they won't hear a word.

Conall. They'll keep it up till the dawn.

Laeg

[Another Charioteer]

[BL(2), 120v]

~~234~~ THE GREEN HELMET

Now it is purring again, and now I drink to your [153–166]
wives,
And I drink to Emer, my wife.
[A great noise without and shouting.
Why, what in God's name is that noise?
***Conall.* What else but the charioteers and the kitchen**
and stable boys
Shouting against each other, and the worst of all is
your own,
That chariot-driver, Laeg, and they'll keep it up till
the dawn,
And there's not a man in the house that will close
his eyes to-night,
Or be able to keep them from it, or know what set
them to fight. *[A noise of horns without.*
There, do you hear them now? Such hatred has each
for each
They have taken the hunting-horns to drown one
another's speech
For fear the truth may prevail.—Here's your good
health and long life
And, though she be quarrelsome, good health to
Emer, your wife.
[The Charioteers, Stable Boys, and Scullions come run-
ning in. They carry great horns, *ladles, and the like.*
***Laeg~~aire~~.* I am Laeg, Cuchulain's driver, and my master's**
cock of the yard.
***Another.* Conall would scatter his feathers.**
[Confused murmurs.
***Laegaire* [*to Cuchulain*]. No use, they won't hear a word.**
***Conall.* They'll keep it up till the dawn.**

and other ~~instruments~~ instruments

what "Another" means—Charioteer or Stable Boy

Laeg

Another Charioteeer {r ?

---

329 Why,] Why *rev to* Why, *NLI 30,006/4*
340 Such] such rev to Such *NLI 30,006/4*
342 hunting-horns] hunting horns *rev to* hunting-horns *NLI 30,006/4*
343 another's] other's *rev to* another's *NLI 30,006/4*
348 Scullions] Kitchen Boys *rev to* Scullions *NLI 30,006/4*
349 horns,] *marginal note inserts* and other instruments *NLI 30,006/4* horns and other instruments *CPl*
350 Laeg~~aire~~] Laegaire *rev to* Laeg *NLI 30,006/4* Laeg *CPl* *marginal note reads* Laeg and Laegaire are different characters *NLI 30,006/4*
352 Another.] Another *marginal note inserts* CHARIOTEER *NLI 30,006/4* Another Charioteer. *CPl*

FIRST PROOF

THE GREEN HELMET 235

Another. It is Laegaire that is the best,
For he fought with cats in Connaught while Conall took his rest
And drained the ale-pot.

Another. Laegaire—what does a man of his sort
Care for the like of us? He did it for his own sport.

Another. It was all mere luck at the best.

Another. But Conall, I say—

Another. Let me speak.

Laegaire. You'd be dumb if the cock of the yard would but open his beak.

Another. Before your cock was born, my master was in the fight.

Laegaire. Go home and praise your grand-dad. They took to the horns for spite,
For I said that no cock of your sort had been born since the fight began.

Another. Conall has got it, the best man has got it, and I am his man.

Cuchulain. Who was it started this quarrel?

A Stable Boy. It was Laeg.

Another. It was Laeg done it all.

Laegaire. A high, wide, foxy man came where we sat in the hall,
Getting our supper ready, with a great voice like the wind,
And cried that there was a helmet, or something of the kind,
That was for the foremost man upon the ridge of the earth.

Q

R. & R. CLARK, Ltd.
6 JUL 1934
EDINBURGH.

[BL(2), 121^{r}]

Marked Proof
Revise

THE GREEN HELMET ~~**235**~~

Another. **It is Laegaire that is the best,** [166–180]
For he fought with cats in Connaught while Conall took his rest Connacht /
And drained ~~the~~ ale-pot. his /
Another. **Laegaire—what does a man of his sort**
Care for the like of us? He did it for his own sport.
Another. **It was all mere luck at the best.**
Another. **But Conall, I say—**
Another. **Let me speak.**
Laeg / ***~~Laegaire~~*****. You'd be dumb if the cock of the yard would but open his beak.**
Another. **Before you cock was born, my master was in the fight.**
~~Should this be Laeg?~~ ***~~Laegaire~~*****. Go home and praise your grand-dad. They took to the horns for spite,**
For I said that no cock of your sort had been born since the fight began.
Another. **Conall has got it, the best man has got it, and I am his man.**
Cuchulain. **Who was it started this quarrel?**
A Stable Boy. **It was Laeg.**
Another. **It was Laeg done it all.**
Laeg ***~~Laegaire~~*****. A high, wide, foxy man came where we sat in the hall,**
Laeg **Getting our supper ready, with a great voice like the wind,**
~~surely~~ **And cried that there was a helmet, or something of the kind,**
That was for the foremost man up on the ride of the earth.

---

356 Another.] Another *marginal note inserts* CHARIOTEER *NLI 30,006/4*
357 Connaught] Connaught *rev to* Connacht *NLI 30,006/4* Connacht *CPl*
359 ~~the~~ ale-pot] his ale pot *rev to* his ale-pot *NLI 30,006/4* his ale-pot *CPl*
365 ~~Laegaire~~] Laegaire *rev to* Laeg *NLI 30,006/4* Laeg *CPl*
369 ~~Laegaire~~] Laegaire *rev to* Laeg *NLI 30,006/4* Laeg *CPl*
378 ~~Laegaire~~] Laegaire *rev to* Laeg *NLI 30,006/4* Laeg *CPl*

[BL(2)]

[121v]

,/ So I cried your name through the hall ^ [181–195]
[*The others cry out and blow horns, partly drowning the rest of his speech.*
but they denied its worth
Preferring Laegaire or Conall, and they cried to drown my voice;
But I have so strong a throat that I drowned all their noise.
Till they took to the hunting-horns and blew them into my face,
And as neither side would give in—we would settle it in this place.
Let the Helmet be taken from Conall.
A Stable Boy. No, Conall is the best man here.
Another. Give it to Laegaire that made the murderous cats pay dear.
Cuchulain. It has been given to none: that our rivalry might cease,
We have turned that murderous cat into a cup of peace.
I drank the first; and then Conall; give it to Laegaire now [*Conall gives Helmet to Laegaire.*
That it may purr in his hand and all of our servants know
,/ That ^ since the ale went in, its claws went out of sight.
A Servant. That's well—I will stop my shouting.
Another. Cuchulain is in the right;
I am tired of this big horn that has made me hoarse as a rook.
Laegaire. Cuchulain, you drank the first.

---

386 hall] hall *rev to* hall, *NLI 30,006/4* hall, *CPl*
394 hunting-horns] hunting horns *rev to* hunting-horns *NLI 30,006/4*
405 peace.] peace, *rev to* peace. *NLI 30,006/4*
407 now] now. *rev to* now *NLI 30,006/4*
410 That since] That since *rev to* That, since *NLI 30,006/4* That, since *CPl*

[122r]

THE GREEN HELMET ~~237~~

Another. **By drinking the first he took** [195–208]
The whole of the honours himself.
Laegaire. **Cuchulain, you drank the first.**
***Another.* If Laegaire drink from it now, he claims to be**
last and worst.
***Another.* Cuchulain and Conall have drunk.**
Another. **He is lost if he taste a drop.**
***Laegaire* [*laying Helmet on table*]. Did you claim to be**
better than us by drinking first from the cup?
Cuchulain* [*his words are partly drowned by the murmurs of
***the crowd though he speaks very loud.*] That juggler**
from the sea, that old red herring it is
Who has set us all by the ears—he brought the
Helmet for this,
And because we would not quarrel he ran elsewhere
to shout
That Conall and Laegair ^ wronged me, till all had e/
fallen out.
[*The murmur grows less so that his words are heard.*
Who knows where he is now or whom he is spurring
to fight. ?
So get you gone, and whatever may cry aloud in the
night,
Or show itself in the air, be silent until morn.
***A Servant.* Cuchulain is in the right—I am tired of this**
big horn.
***Cuchulain.* Go!**
[*The Servants turn towards the door but stop on hearing*
the voices of ~~W~~omen outside. lc
***Laegaire's Wife* [*without*]. Mine is the better to look at.**

---

416 Another.] Another *marginal note inserts then cancels* Charioteer *NLI 30,006/4*
419 now,] now *rev to* now, *NLI 30,006/4*
432 Laegair] Laegaire *NLI 30,006/4, CPl*
435 whom] who *rev to* whom *NLI 30,006/4*
436 fight.] fight. *rev to* fight? *NLI 30,006/4* fight? *CPl*
444 ~~W~~omen] women *CPl*

Conall's Wife [*without*]. But mine is better born.

Emer [*without*]. My man is the pithier man.

Cuchulain. Old hurricane, well done!
You've set our wives to the game that they may egg us on;
We are to kill each other that you may sport with us.
Ah, now they've begun to wrestle as to who'll be first at the house.

[*The Women come to the door struggling.*

Emer. No, I have the right of place for I married the better man.

Conall's Wife [*pulling Emer back*]. My nails in your neck and shoulder.

Laegaire's Wife. And go before me if you can.
My husband fought in the West.

Conall's Wife [*kneeling in the door so as to keep the others out who pull at her*]. But what did he fight with there
But sidelong and spitting and helpless shadows of the dim air?
And what did he carry away but straw and broken delf?

Laegaire's Wife. Your own man made up that tale trembling alone by himself,
Drowning his terror.

Emer [*forcing herself in front*]. I am Emer, it is I go first through the door.
No one shall walk before me, or praise any man before
My man has been praised.

[BL(2), 122v]

~~238~~ THE GREEN HELMET

[208–221]

***Conall's Wife* [*without*]. But mine is better born.**
***Emer* [*without*]. My man is the pithier man.**
***Cuchulain.* Old hurricane, well done!**
You've set our wives to the game that they may egg
us on;
We are to kill each other that you may sport with us.
Ah, now, they're begun to wrestle as to who'll be
first (at) the house. in?
[*The ~~W~~omen come to the door struggling.* lc
***Emer*. No, I have the right of place ^ for I married the**
better man. ,/
***Conall's Wife* [*pulling Emer back*]. My nails in your neck**
and shoulder.
***Laegaire's Wife.* And go before me if you can.**
My husband fought in the West.
Conall's Wife* [*kneeling in the door so as to keep the others out
***who pull at her*]. But what did he fight with there**
But sidelong and spitting and helpless shadows of the
dim air?
And what did he carry away but straw and broken
delf?
***Laegaire's Wife*. Your own man made up that tale**
trembling alone by himself,
Drowning his terror.
***Emer* [*forcing herself in front*]. I am Emer, it is I go first**
through the door.
No one shall walk before me, or praise any man
before close
My man has been praised.

---

452 Ah, now] Ah, now, *rev to* Ah, now *NLI 30,006/4* Ah now, *rev to* Ah, now *BL(1)* Ah, now *CPl*
453 at] at *rev to* in *NLI 30,006/4* in *CPl*
454 ~~W~~omen] women *CPl*
455 place for] place, for *CPl*

---

453 TM's suggested change from "at" to "in" was not marked by WBY, but "in" is the reading of *CPl.*

[BL(2), 123r]

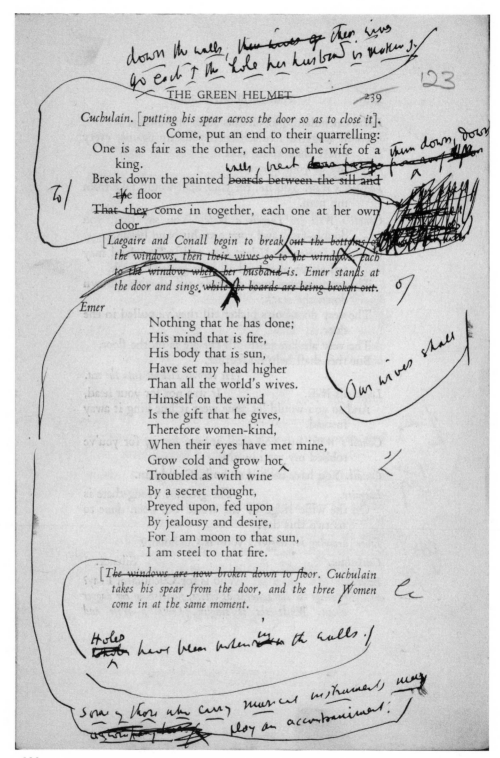

down the walls, their wives
go each to the hole her husband is making./

123

Cuchulain. [*putting his spear across the door so as to close it*].
Come, put an end to their quarrelling:
One is as fair as the other, each one the wife of a king.
Break down the painted ~~boards between the sill and the~~ floor
~~That they~~ come in together, each one at her own door.

[*Laegaire and Conall begin to break* ~~*out the bottoms of the windows, then their wives go to the windows, each to the window where her husband is*~~. *Emer stands at the door and sings*~~, *while the boards are being broken out*~~.

then down, down
walls, break
a

To/

Emer

Nothing that he has done;
His mind that is fire,
His body that is sun,
Have set my head higher
Than all the world's wives.
Himself on the wind
Is the gift that he gives,
Therefore women-kind,
When their eyes have met mine,
Grow cold and grow hot,
Troubled as with wine
By a secret thought,
Preyed upon, fed upon
By jealousy and desire,
For I am moon to that sun,
I am steel to that fire.

Our wives shall

[~~*The windows are now broken down to floor*~~. *Cuchulain takes his spear from the door, and the three Women come in at the same moment.*

Holes have been broken in the walls./

Some of those who carry musical instruments may play an accompaniment./

[BL(2), 123r]

down the walls, ~~their wives go~~ their wives
go each to the hole her husband is making.
THE GREEN HELMET ~~239~~

***Cuchulain.* [*putting his spear across the door so as to close it*].**
Come, put an end to their quarrelling: [221–224]
One is as fair as the other, each one the wife of a
king.
them down, down
walls, break ~~down for fr from roof to floor~~
Break down the painted ~~boards between the sill and~~
to **~~the~~ floor**
~~That they~~ come in together, each one at her own
door.
[*Laegaire and Conall begin to break ~~out the bottoms of~~*
~~the windows, then their wives go to the windows, each~~
~~to the window where her husband is~~. Emer stands at

They shall
~~They shall~~
storm the walls
~~storm the walls~~

Our wives shall

479–486 *the deletions and revisions made to this passage in WBY's hand in BL(2) above are copied into NLI 30,006/4 in the hand of George Yeats*

479–480 ~~boards between the sill and the~~ floor] walls, break them down, down to the floor! *CPl*

481 ~~That they~~] Our wives shall *CPl*

483–484 Laegaire and Conall begin to break down the walls. Their wives go each to the hold her husband is making. *CPl*

479–486 The changes made to this passage represent the only substantive revision to the text of *The Green Helmet* that WBY made after the play first appeared in print in 1910.

[BL(2), 123r]

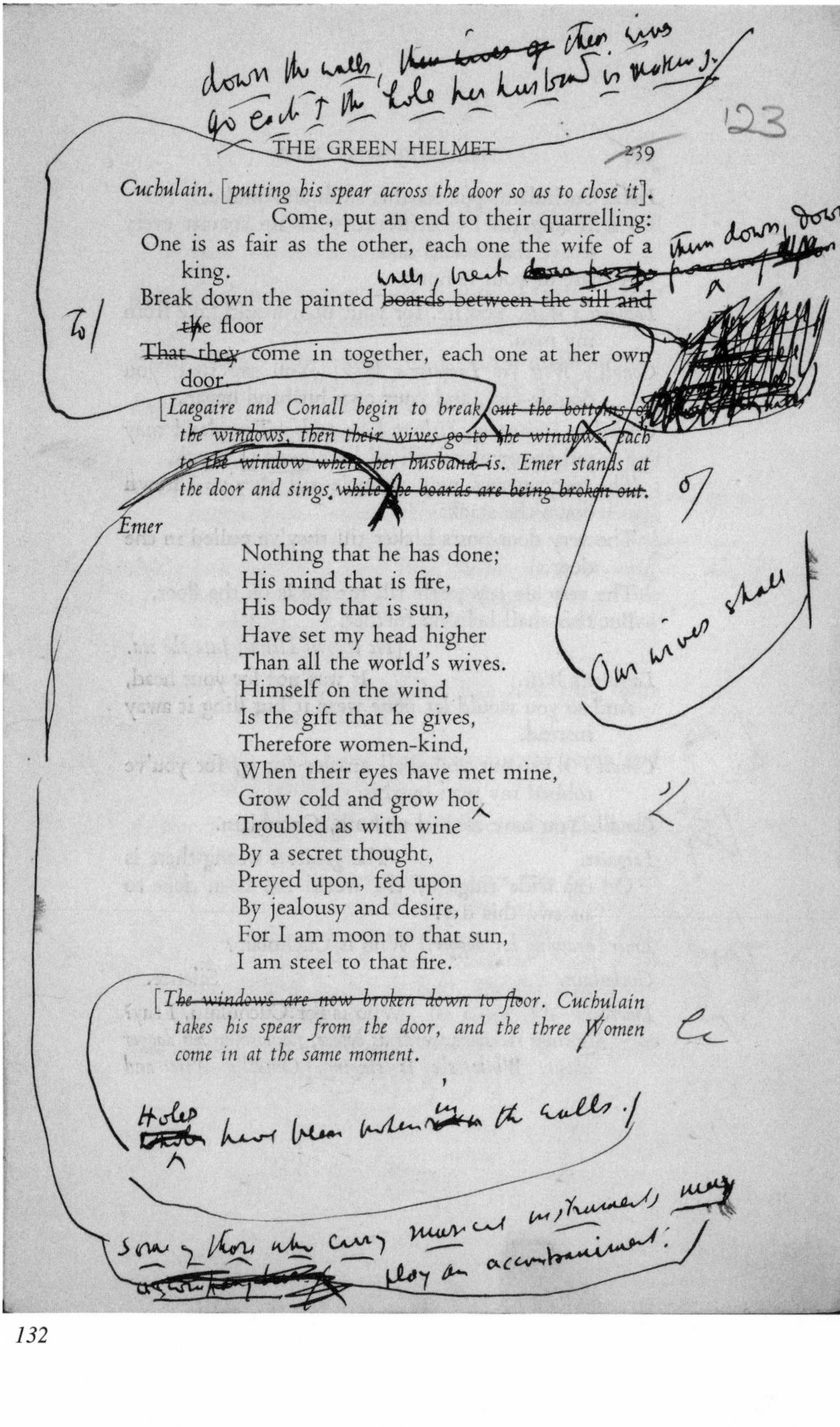

down the walls, ~~then doors of~~ their wives
go each to the hole her husband is making./

123

THE GREEN HELMET 239

Cuchulain. [*putting his spear across the door so as to close it*].
Come, put an end to their quarrelling:
One is as fair as the other, each one the wife of a king.
Break down the painted ~~boards between the sill and the~~ floor
~~That they~~ come in together, each one at her own door
[*Laegaire and Conall begin to break ~~out the bottoms of the windows, then their wives go to the windows, each to the window where her husband is~~. Emer stands at the door and sings ~~while the boards are being broken out~~.*

then down, down
walls, break ~~down pass go pass any upon~~

To/

Our wives shall

Emer
Nothing that he has done;
His mind that is fire,
His body that is sun,
Have set my head higher
Than all the world's wives.
Himself on the wind
Is the gift that he gives,
Therefore women-kind,
When their eyes have met mine,
Grow cold and grow hot,
Troubled as with wine
By a secret thought,
Preyed upon, fed upon
By jealousy and desire,
For I am moon to that sun,
I am steel to that fire.

[*~~The windows are now broken down to floor~~. Cuchulain takes his spear from the door, and the three Women come in at the same moment.*

Holes ~~Doors~~ have been broken in the walls./

Some of those who carry musical instruments may
~~as with many things~~ play an accompaniment./

[BL(2), 123r, continued]

the door and sings, ~~while the boards are being broken out~~.

Emer

Nothing that he has done; [225–240]
His mind that is fire,
His body that is sun,
Have set my head higher
Than all the world's wives.
Himself on the wind Our wives shall
Is the gift that he gives,
Therefore women-kind,
When their eyes have met mine,
Grow cold and grow hot ,
Troubled as with wine
By a secret thought,
Preyed upon, fed upon
By jealousy and desire,
For I am moon to that sun,
I am steel to that fire.

[~~The windows are now broken down to floor~~. Cuchulain takes his spear from the door, and the three ~~W~~omen come in at the same moment. lc

Holes in
~~Wholes~~ have been broken ~~within?~~ the walls.

some of those who carry musical instruments may ~~accompany her~~ play an accompaniment.

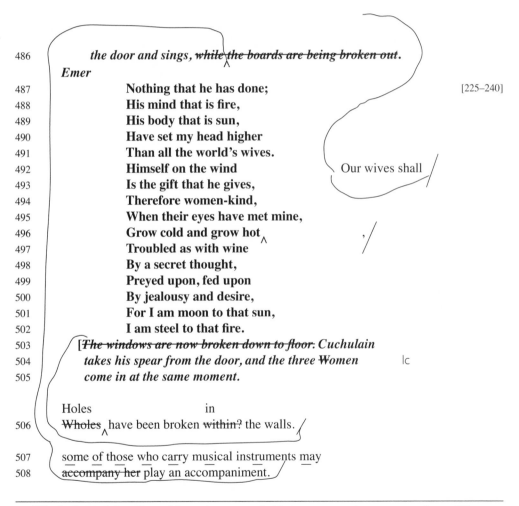

486 the door and sings. Some of those who carry musical instruments may play an accompaniment. *CPl*
496 hot] hot, *CPl*
503 [Holes have been broken in the walls. Cuchulain *CPl*

---

492 The arrow indicates the phrase "Our wives shall" is to replace the canceled words in l. 482 (for the transcription, see pp. 130–131, above).

[BL(2)]

[123^{v}]

Emer. **Cuchulain, put off this sloth and awake:** [241–254]
I will sing till I've stiffened your lip against every
knave that would take
A share of your honour.
Laegaire's Wife. **You lie, for your man would take from**
my man.
Conall's Wife [*to Laegaire's Wife*]. **You say that, you**
double-face, and your own husband began.
Cuchulain [*taking up Helmet from table*]. **Townland may**
rail at townland till all have gone to wrack,
The very straws may wrangle till they've thrown
down the stack;
The very door-posts bicker till they've pulled in the
door,
The very ale-jars jostle till the ale is on the floor,
But this shall help no further.
[*He throws Helmet into the sea.*
Laegaire's Wife. **It was not for your head,**
,/ **And so you would let none wear it** ^ **but fling it away**
instead.
Conall's Wife. **But you shall answer for it, for you've**
robbed my man by this.
tr/ *Conall*. **You have robbed us both, Cucuhlain.**
Laegaire. **The greatest wrong there is**
On the wide ridge of the world has been done to
us two this day.
for/ *Emer* [*drawing her dagger.*] **Who is** ^ **Cuchulain?**
Cuchulain. **Silence.**
Emer. **Who is for Cuchulain, I say?**
[*She sings the same words as before, flourishing her dagger*
about. While she is singing, Conall's Wife and

517–518 Townland may / rail at townland] Town land may rail at town land *rev to* Townland may rail at townland. *Marginal note in the hand of Thomas Mark reads* The word as hitherto *NLI 30,006/4*

527 wear it] wear it *rev to* wear it, *NLI 30,006/4* wear it, *CPl*

531 Cucuhlain] Cuchlain *CPl*

536 Silence.] Silence. *rev to* Silence! *BL(1)*

537 Who is Cuchulain?] Who is for Cuchulain? *NLI 30,006/4, CPl*

539 TM's marks instruct the printer to close up the text.

[124r]

THE GREEN HELMET ~~241~~

Laegaire's Wife draw their daggers and run at her, but Cuchulain forces them back. Laegaire and Conall draw their swords to strike Cuchulain.

Laegaire's Wife [*crying out so as to be heard through Emer's singing*]. Deafen her singing with horns! # [255–259]

Conall's Wife. Cry aloud! blow horns! make a noise!

Laegaire's Wife. Blow horns, clap hands, or shout, so that you smother her voice!

[*The Stable Boys and Scullions blow their horns or fight among themselves. There is a deafening noise and a confused fight. Suddenly three black hands come through the windows and put out the torches. It is now pitch dark, but for a faint light outside the house which merely shows that there are moving forms, but not who or what they are, and in the darkness one can hear low terrified voices.*

A Voice. Coal-black, and headed like cats, they came up over the strand.

Another Voice. And I saw one stretch to a torch and cover it with his hand.

Another Voice. Another sooty fellow has plucked the moon from the air.

[*A light gradually comes into the house from the sea, on which the moon begins to show once more. There is no light within the house, and the great beams of the walls are dark and full of shadows, and the persons of the play dark too against the light. The Red Man is seen standing in the midst of the house. The black cat-headed Men crouch and stand about the door. One carries the Helmet, one the great sword.*

---

548 The Stable Boys] The Horse Boys *rev to* The Stable Boys *NLI 30,006/4*

551 pitch] pitch— *CPl*

567–568 black cat / headed] black cat- / headed *rev to* BLACK CAT- / HEADED *BL(1)*

568 Men] men *CPl*

[BL(2)]

[124v]

Red Man. I demand the debt that's owing. Let some man kneel down there [260–272]
That I may cut his head off, or all shall go to wrack.

Cuchulain. He played and paid with his head ^ and it's right that we pay him back, ,/
And give him more than he gave, for he comes in here as a guest:
So I will give him my head. *[Emer begins to keen.*
Little wife, little wife, be at rest.
the/ ? Alive I have been far off in all lands under sun ^
And been no faithful man; but when my story is done
My fame shall spring up and laugh, and set you high above all.
Emer [*putting her arms around him*]. It is you, not your fame that I love.
Cuchulain [*tries to put her from him*]. You are young, you are wise, you can call
Some kinder and comelier man that will sit at home in the house.
Emer. Live and be faithless still.
Cuchulain [*throwing her from him*]. Would you stay the great barnacle-goose
When its eyes are turned to the sea and its beak to the salt of the air?
Emer [*lifting her dagger to stab herself*]. I, too, on the grey wing's path.
Cuchulain [*seizing dagger*]. Do you dare, do you dare, do you dare?

---

574 head and] head and *rev to* head, and *NLI 30,006/4* head, and *CPl*
580 under sun] under sun *rev to* under the sun *NLI 30,006/4* under the sun *CPl*
597 path.] path! *CPl*

[125^{r}]

THE GREEN HELMET ~~**243**~~

Bear children and sweep the house. [273–284]
[Forcing his way through the servants who gather round.
Wail, but keep from the road.
[He kneels before Red Man. There is a pause.
,/ **Quick to your work, old Radish, you will fade when**
the cocks have crowed.
[A black cat-headed Man holds out the Helmet. The Red
Man takes it.
***Red Man.* I have not come for your hurt, I'm the Rector**
of this land,
Age after age I sift it, and choose ~~from~~ its champion- for/
ship
The man who hits my fancy.
[He places the Helmet on Cuchulain's head.
And I choose the laughing lip
That shall not turn from laughing‸ **whatever rise or** ,/
fall,
The heart that grows no bitterer although betrayed
by all;
The hand that loves to scatter; the life like a
gambler's throw;
And these things I make prosper, till a day come that
I know,
When heart and mind shall darken that the weak
may end the strong,
And the long-remembering harpers have matter for
their song.

~~THE END~~ d

THE END

---

601 servants] servants *rev to* SERVANTS *BL(1)*
606 black cat-headed] black cat-headed *rev to* BLACK CAT-HEADED *BL(1)*
607 Man] men *CPl*
610–611 ~~from~~] for *NLI 30,006/4* for *CPl* champion-/ship] champion-ship *rev to* championship *NLI 30,006/4*
615 laughing] laughing, *CPl*

Appendixes

A. Transcription of Yeats's Note to the Play. NLI 13,571

NLI 13,571 is a nineteen-page typescript of Yeats's notes to his plays, prepared circa 1933 during work on Macmillan's never-published Edition de Luxe. Each play's note occupies a separate page in the typescript. In some cases, as with the note to *The Green Helmet*, the note has simply been cut and pasted from an earlier publication into the 1933 typescript. In the case of the note to *The Green Helmet*, the source is *Plays in Prose and Verse* (London: Macmillan, 1922; Wade 136). This appendix offers a transcription of the note as it reads in the 1933 typescript; editor's notes describe variants from an earlier version of the note that appeared in *Collected Works in Verse and Prose*, vol. 4 (Stratford: Shakespeare Head Press, 1908; Wade 78). Autograph drafts of that earlier note, or of the subsequent revisions made to the note, do not survive.

[NLI 13,571]

A prose version of this play called *The Golden Helmet* was produced at the Abbey Theatre on March 19, 1908, and the present version on February 10, 1910, when Mr. Kerrigan took the part of Cuchulain and Mr. Sinclair and Mr. O'Donovan those of Conall and Leagaire respectively. Miss Allgood, Miss O'Neill, and Miss Magee were the three queens.[1]

In performance we left the black hands to the imagination, and probably when there is so much noise and movement on the stage they would always fail to produce any effect. Our stage is too small to try the experiment, for they would be hidden by the figures of the players. We staged the play with a very pronounced colour-scheme, and I have noticed that the more obviously decorative is the scene and costuming of any play, the more it is lifted out of time and place, and the nearer to faeryland do we carry it. One gets also much more effect out of concerted movements—above all, if there are many players—when all the clothes are the same colour. No breadth of treatment gives monotony when there is movement and change of lighting. It concentrates attention on every new effect and makes every change of outline or of light and shadow surprising and delightful. Because of this one can use contrasts of colour, between clothes and background or in the background itself, the complementary colours for instance, which would be too obvious to keep the attention in a painting. One wishes to make the movement of the action as important as possible, and the simplicity which gives depth of colour does this, just as, for precisely similar reasons, the lack of colour in a statue fixes the attention upon the form.[2]

1911[3]

---

[1]In a version of the note appearing in *Collected Works in Verse and Prose* (1908), the first paragraph reads, "*The Golden Helmet* was produced at the Abbey Theatre on March 19, 1908, with the following cast:—Cuchulain, J. M. Kerrigan; Conal, Arthur Sinclair; Leagerie, Fred. O'Donovan; Laeg, Sydney Morgan; Emer, Sara Allgood; Conal's Wife, Maire O'Neill; Laegerie's Wife, Eileen O'Doherty; Red Man, Ambrose Power; Horseboys, Scullions, and Black Men, S. Hamilton, T. J. Fox, U. Wright, D. Robertson, T. O'Neill, I. A. O'Rourke, P. Kearney."

[2]In the earlier version of the note, a new paragraph was included at the end of the note, reading, "The play is founded upon an old Irish story, *The Feast of Bricriu,* given in *Cuchulain of Muirthemne,* and is meant as an introduction to *On Baile's Strand.*"

[3]The date 1911 was added to the note for its publication in *Plays from an Irish Theatre* (London: A. H. Bullen, 1911; Wade 92).

B. Cast Photographs. NLI 1731

[NLI 1731, p. 34, head]

Scenes from The Golden Helmet
NATIONAL
LIBRARY OF
IRELAND.